THE ECONOMICS OF THE TAX REVOLT: A Reader

ARTHUR B. LAFFER

UNIVERSITY OF SOUTHERN CALIFORNIA

JAN P. SEYMOUR

HARCOURT BRACE JOVANOVICH

New York   San Diego   Chicago   San Francisco   Atlanta

Requests for permission to make copies of any part of the work should be mailed to: Permissions, Harcourt Brace Jovanovich, Inc., 757 Third Avenue, New York, NY 10017.

Printed in the United States of America

Library of Congress Catalog Card Number: 79-84378

ISBN: 0-15-518920-4

CONTENTS

INTRODUCTION   1

1/THE LAFFER CURVE   5

Taxes, Revenues, and the "Laffer Curve"   7
JUDE WANNISKI

An Economic Analysis of the Kemp/Roth Tax Cut Bill, H.R. 8333   13
DONALD W. KIEFER

Vanik's Study Makes Convincing Case for Enactment
of the Kemp-Roth Act   28
JACK KEMP

Alms for the Rich   35
MICHAEL KINSLEY

2/THE KEMP-ROTH BILL   45

The Kemp-Roth-Laffer Free Lunch   46
WALTER HELLER

Populist Remedy for Populist Abuses   50
IRVING KRISTOL

The Real Reasons for a Tax Cut   53
HERBERT STEIN

The Economic Case for Kemp-Roth   57
PAUL CRAIG ROBERTS

Taxes, Inflation, and the Rich   62
MICHAEL K. EVANS

Jack Kemp Wants to Cut Your Taxes—A Lot   65
IRWIN ROSS

3/THE NATIONAL ENERGY PLAN   69

Statement Prepared for the Ad Hoc Energy Committee 71
W. MICHAEL BLUMENTHAL

Statement Prepared for the Joint Economic Committee 75
ARTHUR B. LAFFER

Freedom for Fuel? 80
LOS ANGELES TIMES

Energy Issue Puts Squeeze Play on Carter 82
ERNEST CONINE

4/THE STEIGER-HANSEN BILL   85

Statement Before the Subcommittee on
Taxation and Debt Management 86
OTTO ECKSTEIN

Economic and Investment Observations:
Capital Gains Tax Rate Reduction 95
ARTHUR B. LAFFER

Statement Before the Subcommittee on
Taxation and Debt Management 99
W. MICHAEL BLUMENTHAL

Inflation and Capital Formation 106
MARTIN FELDSTEIN

5/PROPOSITION 13—
THE JARVIS-GANN INITIATIVE   109

Proposition 13: Its Impact on the Nation's Economy,
Federal Revenues, and Federal Expenditures 110
CONGRESSIONAL BUDGET OFFICE

Punching Through the Jarvis Myth 114
WILLIAM SCHNEIDER

The Jarvis-Gann Tax Cut Proposal:
An Application of the Laffer Curve 118
CHARLES W. KADLEC AND ARTHUR B. LAFFER

"Meat-Axe Radicalism" in California 123
WALTER HELLER

Aftershocks from the Great California Taxquake 126
JOHN QUIRT

Voting for Capitalism 134
JOHN A. DAVENPORT

INTRODUCTION

This book of readings offers a series of position papers and chronologies on five of the primary focal points of the so-called "tax revolution in America": the Laffer Curve, the Kemp-Roth bill, the National Energy Plan, the Steiger-Hansen amendment, and Proposition 13. The intention is simply to provide a balanced and representative sample of the economic debate of 1978.

The catalysts for this debate, which originated in the political arena, were provided by such people as Congressmen Jack Kemp and William Steiger; Senators William Roth and Clifford Hansen; political reformers Howard Jarvis and Paul Gann; and Jude Wanniski, who fueled the debate in his writings on the editorial page of *The Wall Street Journal* and in his controversial book *The Way the World Works: How Economies Fail and Succeed* (published by Basic Books, 1978). The debate was quickly joined by economists from the entire spectrum of current economic thought.

Postwar macroeconomics has witnessed the emergence of two competing aggregate demand theories. While both monetarists and Keynesians can trace their intellectual heritages far into the past, they had never previously attained anything close to the predominance that they have experienced during the past thirty years. Prior to their emergence as the dominant intellectual force, classical theory was the stock in trade of the profession. In the Western world the successes of aggregate demand theories were accompanied by the nearly complete disappearance of classical thought. However, even the fierce competition between Marxist and laissez-faire economics has never extended to a serious questioning of the primal importance of individual economic incentives, which is the basic tenet of classicism.

Monetarists and Keynesians agree, in principle, that shifts in aggregate demand are the major source of changes in output, employment, and the price level. Their disagreements center primarily on the relative importance of monetary, fiscal, and international economic policies in influencing aggregate demand. For the monetarist, changes in aggregate demand depend primarily on changes in the growth rate of the money supply. Fiscalists, on the other hand, focus primarily on the aggregate demand impact of total government spending, total tax receipts, and the budget deficit. For both Keynesians and monetarists unanimity is achieved in regard to the importance of

1

the effects of exchange rate policies on aggregate demand. They also agree that the trade-off between inflation and increased output resulting from an increase in demand directly depends upon the degree of capacity utilization in the economy. Given an increase in aggregate demand, the greater the utilization of current capacity, the greater will be the increase in prices and the smaller the increase in output.

In the context of the current U.S. economy, Keynesians and monetarists alike see capacity constraints looming. The increase in total employment and the changing composition of the labor force portray a picture of labor supply bottlenecks. Plant capacity utilization also appears to be high. Therefore, within the context of an aggregate demand model, tax rate reductions, while leading to increases in aggregate demand, will not result in correspondingly large increases in supply. Deficits will increase.

Monetarists argue that to the extent these deficits are financed by money creation, inflation will increase; more money will be chasing essentially the same number of goods. Keynesians, too, see larger deficits and greater inflation. The Keynesian argument, however, hinges more on the pure increase in aggregate demand accompanied by supply constraints than it does on accommodative money increases.

Nonetheless, a number of monetarists support policies to reduce tax rates. They base their case on the proposition that less revenues to the government will force a reduction in government spending. Government spending reductions being the benefit and inflation being the cost, several monetarist-oriented economists come out in favor of tax rate reductions while others oppose them.

Modern classical economists take an entirely different tack from exclusively demand-oriented analysis. The driving force of the economy is the incentive to engage in market-oriented activities. In both the long run as well as the short run, individuals and groups of individuals allocate resources according to after-tax yields. If market activities are profitable, the economy will shun leisure and other nonmarket ventures while concentrating on ever-increasing market successes. If, however, successful market performance encounters waxing discrimination in the forms of high and progressive taxes, regulations, and other forms of societal disapprobation, economic activity will subside.

Within the classical framework a production-oriented tax rate reduction increases incentives and leads to an expansion in output. The tax rate reduction increases supply incentives and thereby potential, as well as actual output. Capacity constraints, as such, depend upon the incentives. An increase in incentives raises potential output. Therefore, the notion of a capacity constraint does not play a role within the classical framework.

The effects of a tax rate reduction on inflation, output, employment, and even the deficit depend critically upon supply responses. In addition to the pure supply responses, tax revenues will also be affected by tax evasion and avoidance incentives as well as the allocation of productive resources. With lower tax rates there will be less advantage to evade or avoid the payment of taxes. Real resources will be freed as well as more efficiently allocated to the final endeavor of yielding output. The argument continues that the path of government spending will even be lowered as a result of more rapid real growth.

As often as not a cut in tax rates will lower deficits. With more goods and less deficit financing, inflation will fall. For classical analysis, correctly constituted tax rate reductions do provide the proverbial "free lunch."

These views as well as many of their sources are contained in the diverse readings in this book.

We would like to thank Edith Trimble and Mary Gavin for their expert help on this book. Another person who enormously benefited this project was the late Congressman William Steiger, without whose efforts much of the debate would never have existed. It is in his memory that the book is dedicated.

1/
THE LAFFER CURVE

The lowering of tax rates has two revenue effects, as explained by Arthur B. Laffer. These effects are the arithmetic effect and the economic effect. The first effect is the one that comes to mind most readily. If tax rates are lowered, tax revenues will be lower by the amount of decrease in the rate multiplied by the tax base. This, of course, assumes no change in the tax base. The economic effect, however, recognizes the positive impact lower taxes have on work, saving, and investment by providing incentives to increase these activities. Accordingly, lowering tax rates may lead to increased economic activity, an expanded tax base, and, therefore, increased tax revenues.

This is the basic theory behind the Laffer Curve, so named by Jude Wanniski in his book *The Way the World Works: How Economies Fail and Succeed* and used by Laffer to illustrate the relationship between tax rates and government revenues. The curve shows that there are two tax rates that yield the same level of revenues to the government—one is high and one is low. As tax rates decline from the prohibitively high range, government revenues actually increase from expanded economic growth.

Laffer does not claim to have invented the curve; the theory has been around for a long time. The fourteenth century Arabic philosopher Ibn Khaldun discusses this concept in *The Muqaddimah* in the chapter titled "Taxation and the Reason for High and Low Tax Revenues," a portion of which is excerpted below:

> It should be known that at the beginning of the dynasty, taxation yields a large revenue from small assessments. At the end of the dynasty, taxation yields a small revenue from large assessments. . . .
>
> Often, when the decrease is noticed, the amounts of individual imposts are increased. . . . The costs of all cultural enterprises are now too high; the taxes are too heavy, and the profits anticipated fail to materialize. . . . Finally, civilization is destroyed, because the incentive for cultural activity is gone. . . .[1]

---

[1]"Notable and Quotable," *The Wall Street Journal*, September 29, 1978, p. 20, as quoted from Franz Rosenthal, trans., *The Muqaddimah*, Princeton University Press Bollingen Series, XLVIII, Vol. 2, 1967.

In 1879, Henry George—writer, economist, and philosopher—discussed in his book *Progress and Poverty* the importance of utilizing the proper mode of taxation, which is another component of the Laffer theory. He wrote:

> But the manner in which equal amounts of taxation may be imposed may very differently affect the production of wealth. Taxation which lessens the reward of the producer necessarily lessens the incentive to production; taxation which is conditioned upon the act of production, or the use of any of the three factors of production necessarily discourages production.[2]

Laffer's tax cut theory is cited by supporters of the various tax cut measures on the state and federal levels. It has been both praised and attacked by politicians, business people, academicians, and the media. Some varied viewpoints and applications of the Laffer Curve follow.

[2]Henry George, *Poverty and Progress* (New York: Robert Schalkenbach Foundation, 1939), p. 409.

Taxes, Revenues, and the "Laffer Curve"

JUDE WANNISKI

Jude Wanniski, formerly an associate editor of *The Wall Street Journal* and currently a private consultant, describes the Laffer Curve as it applies to American economic and political history, as well as to several foreign governments.

As Arthur Laffer has noted, "There are always two tax rates that yield the same revenues." When an aide to President Gerald Ford asked him once to elaborate, Laffer . . . drew a simple curve, shown on the next page, to illustrate his point. The point, too, is simple enough—though, like so many simple points, it is also powerful in its implications.

When the tax rate is 100 percent, all production ceases in the money economy (as distinct from the barter economy, which exists largely to escape taxation). People will not work in the money economy if all the fruits of their labors are confiscated by the government. And because production ceases, there is nothing for the 100-percent rate to confiscate, so government revenues are zero.

On the other hand, if the tax rate is zero, people can keep 100 percent of what they produce in the money economy. There is no governmental "wedge" between earnings and after-tax income, and thus no governmental barrier to production. Production is therefore maximized, and the output of the money economy is limited only by the desire of workers for leisure. But because the tax rate is zero, government revenues are again zero, and there can be no government. So at a 0-percent tax rate the economy is in a state of anarchy, and at a 100-percent tax rate the economy is functioning entirely through barter.

In between lies the curve. If the government reduces its rate to something less than 100 percent, say to point A, some segment of the barter economy will be able to gain so many efficiencies by being in the money economy that, even with near-confiscatory tax rates, after-tax production would still exceed that of the barter economy. Production will start up, and revenues will flow into the government treasury. By lowering the tax rate, we find an increase in revenues.

On the bottom end of the curve, the same thing is happening. If people feel that they need a minimal government and thus institute a low tax rate, some segment of the economy, finding that the marginal loss of income exceeds the efficiencies gained in the money economy, is shifted into either barter or leisure.

Jude Wanniski, "Taxes, Revenues, and the 'Laffer Curve,' " *The Public Interest*, Winter 1978, pp. 3–16. Reprinted by permission of the author.

This article is adapted from the author's book *The Way the World Works: How Economies Fail and Succeed* (Basic Books, 1978).

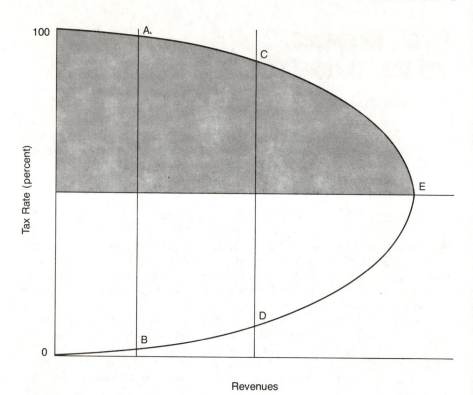

THE LAFFER CURVE

But with that tax rate, revenues do flow into the government treasury. This is the situation at point B. Point A represents a very high tax rate and very low production. Point B represents a very low tax rate and very high production. Yet they both yield the same revenue to the government.

The same is true of points C and D. The government finds that by a further lowering of the tax rate, say from point A to point C, revenues increase with the further expansion of output. And by raising the tax rate, say from point B to point D, revenues also increase, by the same amount.

Revenues and production are maximized at point E. If, at point E, the government lowers the tax rate again, output will increase, but revenues will fall. And if, at point E, the tax rate is raised, both output and revenue will decline. The shaded area is *the prohibitive range for government*, where rates are unnecessarily high and can be reduced with gains in *both* output and revenue.

TAX RATES AND TAX REVENUES

The next important thing to observe is that, except for the 0-percent and 100-percent rates, there are no numbers along the "Laffer curve." Point E is not 50 percent, although it may be, but rather a variable number: *It is the point at which the electorate desires to be taxed.* At points B and D, the electorate desires more government goods and services and is willing—without reducing its productivity—to pay the higher rates consistent with the revenues at point E. And at points A and C, the electorate desires more private goods and services in the money economy, and wishes to pay the lower rates consistent with the revenues at point E. It is the task of the statesman to determine the location of point E, and follow its variations as closely as possible.

This is true whether the political leader heads a nation or a family. The father who disciplines his son at point A, imposing harsh penalties for violating both major and minor rules, only invites sullen rebellion, stealth, and lying (tax evasion, on the national level). The permissive father who disciplines casually at point B invites open, reckless rebellion: His son's independence and relatively unfettered growth come at the expense of the rest of the family. The wise parent seeks point E, which will probably vary from one child to another, from son to daughter.

For the political leader on the national level, point E can represent a very low or a very high number. When the nation is at war, point E can approach 100 percent. At the siege of Leningrad in World War II, for example, the people of the city produced for 900 days at tax rates approaching 100 percent. Russian soldiers and civilians worked to their physical limits, receiving as "pay" only the barest of rations. Had the citizens of Leningrad not wished to be taxed at that high rate, which was required to hold off the Nazi army, the city would have fallen.

The number represented by point E will change abruptly if the nation is at war one day and at peace the next. The electorate's demand for military goods and services from the government will fall sharply; the electorate will therefore desire to be taxed at a lower rate. If rates are not lowered consistent with this new lower level of demand, output will fall to some level consistent with a point along the prohibitive side of the "Laffer curve." Following World War I, for example, the wartime tax rates were left in place and greatly contributed to the recession of 1919–20. Warren G. Harding ran for President in 1920 on a slogan promising a "return to normalcy" regarding tax rates; he was elected in a landslide. The subsequent rolling back of the rates ushered in the economic expansion of the "Roaring Twenties." After World War II, wartime tax rates were quickly reduced, and the American economy enjoyed a smooth transition to peacetime. In Japan and West Germany, however, there was no adjustment of the rates; as a result, postwar economic recovery was delayed. Germany's recovery began in 1948, when personal income-tax rates were reduced under Finance Minister Ludwig Erhard, and much of the government regulation of commerce came to an end. Japan's recovery did not begin until 1950, when wartime tax rates were finally rolled back. In each case, reduced *rates* produced increased *revenues* for the government. The political leader must fully appreciate the distinction between tax rates and tax revenues to discern the desires of the electorate.

The easiest way for a political leader to determine whether an increase in rates will produce more rather than less revenues is to put the proposition to the electorate. It is not enough for the politician to propose an increase from, say, point B to point D on the curve. He must also specify how the anticipated revenues will be spent. When voters approve a bond issue for schools, highways, or bridges, they are explicitly telling the politician that they are willing to pay the high tax rates required to finance the bonds. In rejecting a bond issue, however, the electorate is not necessarily telling the politician that taxes are already high enough, or that point E (or beyond) has been reached. The only message is that the proposed tax rates are too high a price to pay for the specific goods and services offered by the government.

Only a tiny fraction of all government expenditures are determined in this fashion, to be sure. Most judgments regarding tax rates and expenditures are made by individual politicians. Andrew Mellon became a national hero for engineering the rate reductions of the 1920's, and was called "the greatest Treasury Secretary since Alexander Hamilton." The financial policies of Ludwig Erhard were responsible for what was hailed as "an economic miracle"—the postwar recovery of Germany. Throughout history, however, it has been the exception rather than the rule that politicians, by accident or design, have sought to increase revenues by lowering rates. . . .

THE POLITICS OF THE "LAFFER CURVE"

The "Laffer curve" is a simple but exceedingly powerful analytical tool. In one way or another, all transactions, even the simplest, take place along it. The homely adage, "You can catch more flies with molasses than with vinegar," expresses the essence of the curve. But empires are built on the bottom of this simple curve and crushed against the top of it. The Caesars understood this, and so did Napoleon (up to a point) and the greatest of the Chinese emperors. The Founding Fathers of the United States knew it well; the arguments for union (in *The Federalist Papers*) made by Hamilton, Madison, and Jay reveal an understanding of the notion. Until World War I—when progressive taxation was sharply increased to help finance it—the United States successfully remained out of the "prohibitive range."

In the 20th century, especially since World War I, there has been a constant struggle by all the nations of the world to get down the curve. The United States managed to do so in the 1920's, because Andrew Mellon understood the lessons of the "Laffer curve" for the domestic economy. Mellon argued that there are always two prices in the private market that will produce the same revenues. Henry Ford, for example, could get the same revenue by selling a few cars for $100,000 each, or a great number for $1,000 each. (Of course, Ford was forced by the threat of competition to sell at the low price.) The tax rate, said Mellon, is the "price of government." But the nature of government is monopolistic; government itself must find the lowest rate that yields the desired revenue.

Because Mellon was successful in persuading Republican Presidents—first Warren G. Harding and then Calvin Coolidge— of the truth of his ideas the high wartime tax rates were steadily cut back. The excess-profits tax on industry was repealed, and the 77-percent rate on the highest bracket of personal income was rolled back in stages, so that by 1925 it stood at 25 percent. As a result, the period 1921–29 was one of phenomenal economic expansion: G.N.P. grew from $69.6 billion to $103.1 billion. And because prices fell during this period, G.N.P. grew even faster in real terms, by 54 percent. At the lower rates, revenues grew sufficiently to enable Mellon to reduce the national debt from $24.3 billion to $16.9 billion.

The stock market crash of 1929 and the subsequent global depression occurred because Herbert Hoover unwittingly contracted the world economy with his high-tariff policies, which pushed the West, as an economic unit, up the "Laffer curve." Hoover compounded the problem in 1932 by raising personal tax rates almost up to the levels of 1920.

The most important economic event following World War II was also the work of a finance minister who implicitly understood the importance of the "Laffer curve." Germany had been pinned to the uppermost ranges of the curve since World War I. It took a financial panic in the spring of 1948 to shake Germany loose. At that point, German citizens were still paying a 50-percent marginal tax rate on incomes of $600 and a 95-percent rate on incomes above $15,000. On June 22, 1948, Finance Minister Ludwig Erhard announced cuts that raised the 50 percent bracket to $2,200 and the 95-percent bracket to $63,000. The financial panic ended, and economic expansion began. It was Erhard, not the Marshall Plan, who saved Europe from Communist encroachment. In the decade that followed, Erhard again and again slashed the tax rates, bringing the German economy farther down the curve and into a higher level of prosperity. In 1951 the 50-percent bracket was pushed up to $5,000 and in 1953 to $9,000, while at the same time the rate for the top bracket was reduced to 82 percent. In 1954, the rate for the top bracket was reduced again, to 80 percent, and in 1955 it was pulled down sharply, to 63 percent on incomes above $250,000; the 50-percent bracket was pushed up to $42,000. Yet another tax reform took place in 1958: The government exempted the first $400 of income and brought the rate for the top bracket down to 53 percent. It was this systematic lowering of unnecessarily high tax rates that produced the German "economic miracle." As national income rose in Germany throughout the 1950's, so did revenues, enabling the government to construct its "welfare state" as well as its powerful national defense system.

The British empire was built on the lower end of the "Laffer curve" and dismantled on the upper end. The high wartime rates imposed to finance the Napoleonic wars were cut back sharply in 1816, despite warnings from "fiscal experts" that the high rates were needed to reduce the enormous public debt of £900 million. For the following 60 years, the British economy grew at an unprecedented pace, as a series of finance ministers used ever-expanding revenues to lower steadily the tax rates and tariffs.

In Britain, though, unlike the United States, there was no Mellon to risk lowering the extremely high tax rates imposed to finance World War I. As a result, the British economy struggled through the 1920's and 1930's. After World War II, the British government again made the mistake of not sufficiently lowering tax rates to spur individual initiative. Instead, the postwar Labour government concentrated on using tax policy for Keynesian objectives—i.e., increasing consumer demand to expand output. On October 23, 1945, tax rates were cut on lower-income brackets and surtaxes were added to the already high rates on the upper-income brackets. Taxes on higher incomes were increased, according to Chancellor of the Exchequer Hugh Dalton, in order to "continue that steady advance toward economic and social equality which we have made during the war and which the Government firmly intends to continue in peace."

From that day in 1945, there has been no concerted political voice in Britain arguing for a reduction of the high tax rates. Conservatives have supported and won tax reductions for business, especially investment-tax income credits. But while arguing for a reduction of the 83-percent rate on incomes above £20,000 (roughly $35,000 at current exchange rates) of earned income and the 98-percent rate on "unearned income" from investments, they have insisted that government *first* lower its spending, in order to permit the rate reductions. Somehow, the spending levels never can be cut. Only in the last several months of 1977 has Margaret Thatcher, the leader of the opposition Conservative Party, spoken of reducing the high tax rates as a way of expanding revenues.

In the United States, in September 1977, the Republican National Committee unanimously endorsed the plan of Representative Jack Kemp of New York for cutting tax rates as a way of expanding revenues through increased business activity. This was the first time since 1953 that the GOP had embraced the concept of tax cuts! In contrast, the Democrats under President Kennedy sharply cut tax rates in 1962–64 (though making their case in Keynesian terms). The reductions successfully moved the United States economy down the "Laffer curve," expanding the economy and revenues.

It is crucial to Western economic expansion, peace, and prosperity that "conservative" parties move in this direction. They are, after all, traditionally in favor of income growth, with "liberals" providing the necessary political push for income redistribution. A welfare state is perfectly consistent with the "Laffer curve," and can function successfully along its lower range. But there must be income before there can be income redistribution. Most of the economic failures of this century can rightly be charged to the failure of conservatives to press for tax rates along the lower range of the "Laffer curve." Presidents Eisenhower, Nixon and Ford were timid in this crucial area of public policy. The Goldwater Republicans of 1963–64, in fact, emphatically opposed the Kennedy tax rate cuts!

If, during the remainder of this decade, the United States and Great Britain demonstrate the power of the "Laffer curve" as an analytical tool, its use will spread, in the developing countries as well as the developed world. Politicians who understand the curve will find that they can defeat politicians who do not, other things being equal. Electorates all over the world always know when they are unnecessarily perched along the upper edge of the "Laffer curve," and will support political leaders who can bring them back down.

An Economic Analysis of the Kemp/Roth Tax Cut Bill, H.R. 8333

DONALD W. KIEFER

The Library of Congress, at the request of Congressman Charles A. Vanik of Ohio, completed a study on the Kemp-Roth tax cut bill, which was included in the *Congressional Record* of August 2, 1978. In the study, Donald W. Kiefer, a specialist in taxation and fiscal policy, specifically criticizes (1) the use of the Kennedy tax cuts and the subsequent economic boom as support for the Kemp-Roth bill and (2) the Laffer Curve theory as it applies to the bill.

The "Tax Reduction Act of 1977," H.R. 8333,[1] better known as the Kemp/Roth tax cut bill, has become the subject of substantial interest in Congress and the nation at large in mid-1978. The bill and its underlying philosophy, largely embodied in the so-called "Laffer Curve," have been the subject of considerable Congressional discussion and debate, numerous articles in the popular press and programs in the electronic media, and a large number of requests to the Congressional Research Service for information and analysis. This paper is intended as an overall response to those requests and, in part, incorporates material from prior CRS memoranda and reports. The analysis is organized into three sections: 1) a description of the bill and its direct economic effects, 2) an analysis of the supporting arguments for the bill, and 3) a discussion of the available estimates of the bill's potential macroeconomic effects.

DESCRIPTION OF THE TAX CUTS IN THE KEMP/ROTH BILL AND THEIR DIRECT ECONOMIC EFFECTS

H.R. 8333 would cut individual and corporate income through three separate devices, all conceptually simple. Individual income taxes would be cut through reductions in statutory tax rates applicable to each taxable income bracket. Corporate income taxes would be reduced by a cut in the normal corporate tax rates and an increase in the surtax exemption. . . .

AN ANALYSIS OF THE SUPPORTING ARGUMENTS FOR THE KEMP/ROTH TAX CUT

While the proponents of the Kemp/Roth bill have advanced a number of arguments on its behalf, two contentions have received the principal emphasis and

[1]The bill was introduced July 14, 1977, and proposes tax cuts beginning in calendar 1978. For analytical purposes this paper assumes the tax cuts would still begin in 1978 even though nearly a year has passed since its introduction.

Donald W. Kiefer, "An Economic Analysis of the Kemp/Roth Tax Cut Bill, H.R. 8333: A Description, an Examination of Its Rationale, and Estimates of Its Economic Effects," *Congressional Record*, August 2, 1978, pp. H7777–H7787.

gained the most attention. The first involves reference to the 1964 tax cut as an appropriate historical precedent for the Kemp/Roth bill, and the second is the assertion that a general tax cut can be self-financing.[2] The latter argument usually includes a reference, in name or in substance, to the so-called "Laffer Curve."

With regard to the 1964 tax cut the Kemp/Roth advocates have advanced essentially four propositions: (1) that there is a strong analogy between the economic conditions in 1964 and at the present, (2) that the 1964 tax cut was a successful fiscal policy worthy of emulation, (3) that the economic "feedback effects" of the 1964 tax cut were completely unanticipated, and (4) that the increase in tax revenue which was generated by the more rapid economic activity resulting from the 1964 tax cut more than offset the original revenue loss attributable to the tax cut. . . .

The "Laffer Curve" and Supply Side Fiscal Response

The general contention that a sizeable tax cut will have large supply side effects through stronger incentives to work, save, and invest has most often been voiced by the Kemp/Roth proponents through reference to the so-called "Laffer Curve," named for its originator, Professor Arthur Laffer of the University of Southern California. The most extensive presentation of the Laffer Curve has been made by Jude Wanniski in ["Taxes, Revenues, and the 'Laffer Curve'"]. . . .

Laffer Curve adherents, including Professor Laffer, argue that the United States is now in the "prohibitive range" of taxation. This claim and [Wanniski's] description are the rationale for arguing that the Kemp/Roth tax cut, or presumably any tax cut, would increase Government revenue rather than reduce it.

The Laffer Curve obviously has a certain amount of intuitive appeal. However, it is also an overly simplistic approach which ignores very complex economic relationships, and therefore falls considerably short of providing information directly relevant to policy formulation. A brief analytical review of the concept is provided below in outline format.

1. Central to the Laffer Curve is the notion that there is something which can be called a "tax rate" for the overall economy, and that for each tax rate a given amount of tax revenue will be raised. But what is this tax rate? There are literally hundreds of different taxes imposed by the Federal Government and State and local governments; they apply to personal income, corporate income, wages, sales, property, and myriad other tax bases. Their structures vary; some are flat-rate taxes; some have elaborate exemptions and deductions. It is impossible for one tax rate to characterize this complex tax structure in the U.S.

Even if one decided to use one effective tax rate—say total tax revenue divided by GNP, or total personal taxes divided by personal income—major oversimplification would still be a problem. The association of a single amount of revenue with each tax rate implies that the type of tax mechanism used to raise the revenue is irrelevant; i.e. whether the tax is imposed on consumption, or wealth, or income, or only income from capital, and whether the tax is regressive, proportional, or progressive do not matter in determining the

[2]See, for example, the introductory statements of Mr. Kemp and Mr. Roth, *Congressional Record*, 95th Congress, 1st Session, July 14, 1977, pp. H7156–H7158, and S11899–S11901, respectively.

economic effects of the tax and the revenue it will yield. The Laffer Curve implies all that matters is the undefined "tax rate." However, this is an over-simplification which is contradicted by virtually all of public finance analysis, and, indeed, is also contradicted by other arguments offered by the Laffer Curve adherents (see point 7 below).

2. The Laffer Curve represents a gross simplification of a major portion of macroeconomics into a single curved line. Countless books and articles have been written to conceptualize, identify, and measure the impact of taxation and fiscal policy on the U.S. economy, and despite all of this effort and research there are still many important issues which are unresolved. However, it is known that the effect of a tax cut or tax increase on the economy, and in turn on tax revenues, depends on a multitude of factors and their complex interrelationships. These factors include the level of employment and unemployment, the level of capacity utilization, the level of investment, interest rates, inflation rates, the savings rate, the posture of monetary policy, levels of consumer and business confidence, the size of the Federal deficit, the budget position of State and local governments, and the level of the foreign trade balance, to name only a few. Additionally, for many variables—for example capacity utilization and investment—it is important to view them both in the aggregate and disaggregated by economic sector and region. Also, since economic phenomena are dynamic, it is important to know the trends of the economic indicators as well as their levels; a 6 percent unemployment rate does not mean the same thing if the trend is upward as if the trend is downward.

All of these factors and many more are involved in understanding and assessing the potential economic impact of a tax cut. To subsume all of these economic effects into a single line on a graph is to ignore much of the substance of responsible tax policy.

3. The notion behind the Laffer Curve depends almost entirely on the response of work, savings, and investment behavior to levels of taxation. The assertion is that higher taxes lead to reduced incentives and lower levels of economic activity; lower taxes increase incentives and economic activity. The Laffer Curve asserts that as taxes are increased from 0 to 100 percent, at some point the effect on tax revenue of the diminished economic activity overwhelms the effect of the higher tax rates, and tax revenue begins decreasing rather than increasing. This assertion is no doubt true, but because the Laffer analysis concentrates on economic responses at or near the end points—tax rates of 0 and 100 percent—it is not very relevant. The relevant issue is the incentive effect of small tax rate changes within the range of feasible alternatives to present policy. Analysis of these incentive effects is much more complex and leads to different conclusions than suggested by the Laffer Curve.

The Laffer Curve ignores the fact that within the relevant range of policy alternatives, tax rate changes induce two reactions, an income effect and a substitution effect, which tend to offset each other. Richard and Peggy Musgrave, in their well known public finance textbook, describe and assess these factors with regard to work effort as follows:

"With regard to labor, we shall find that introduction of an income tax need not reduce hours of work. To be sure, the tax results in a reduction in the net wage rate. This makes work less attractive relative to leisure and induces workers to work less (the so-called substitution effect). But a tax also makes them poorer, so they tend to feel that they cannot afford as much leisure and must work more (the so-called income effect). Depending on which consideration carries more weight, effort may rise or fall. Such empirical evidence as is available gives little support to either hypothesis but suggests that labor supply to the economy as a whole is fairly inelastic to the wage rate."[3]

And further in a later passage:

"If the labor supply schedule is upward-sloping, as most textbooks draw it, the negative substitution effect outweighs the positive income effect; if the schedule is backward-sloping, the opposite response occurs.

"Historically, it is evident that rising wage rates have been accompanied by reduced hours of work, i.e. a substantial part of the gains from productivity growth has been directed into increased leisure. Although this does not prove that the short-run supply schedule of labor is backward-sloping (in which case taxation would raise, rather than lower, the amount of labor supplied), it should not be readily assumed that an income tax must reduce effort. While we all seem to know someone who has been discouraged by taxation and has worked less, most of us seem to respond by working more.

"As noted before, much depends on the rate schedule. A person will work less under a progressive than under a proportional rate schedule, if the same amount is drawn from him in both cases. Yet, work effort for taxpayers as a group need not be lower under a progressive schedule. The net effect depends on how wage earners at various points on the income scale respond. Earners at the upper end (where rates will be higher than under a proportional tax of equal yield) have more flexibility in hours worked but may also be less responsive to changes in the net wage rate, since other forms of motivation (prestige, interest in work, etc.) may dominate. Employees at the lower end of the scale have less flexibility in their work effort responses and also face lower marginal rates of income tax. The most serious problem of disincentive to work may well occur below the income tax range where welfare policies are such as to imply high marginal rates of tax on earned income."[4]

. . . The Musgrave analysis reveals that the effect of the income tax on household saving and on investment is uncertain; the effect on business saving, however, is negative assuming the corporate income tax is borne by capital. Some recent econometric research concludes that the impact of the tax structure on the rate of savings is more significant than has been previously thought,[5] but even these new results are of a small magnitude compared to that required to support the Laffer Curve hypothesis. Thus, the notions of the effects of taxation on incentives embodied in the Laffer Curve are considerably oversimplified and exaggerated.

4. By concentrating primarily on incentive and supply side effects, the Laffer Curve largely ignores the actual mechanism by which fiscal policy exerts its biggest and most immediate impact—demand side effects. The most immediate impact of a tax cut is that individuals and businesses have more disposable or after tax income. The largest percentage of this after tax income will be spent

---

[3]Musgrave, Richard A. and Peggy B. Musgrave, *Public Finance in Theory and Practice*, Second Edition, McGraw-Hill Book Company, New York, 1973. p. 407.
[4]Ibid. pp. 484–485
[5]See for example, Boskin, Michael J., Taxation, Saving, and the Rate of Interest, *Journal of Political Economy*. Volume 86, No. 2, Part 2, April 1978, pp. S3–S27.

rather rapidly, thus raising aggregate demand in the economy. If there are unemployed workers and idle productive resources, this higher aggregate demand will lead to more jobs and higher GNP; if unemployment is slight and there is little idle capacity, the increased demand will be inflationary and destabilizing.

Thus, the timing of a tax cut is very important. However, the Laffer Curve analysis does not include an explicit consideration of the state of the economy at the time of a tax cut. It asserts that we are in the "prohibitive range" of taxation, and offers the faith that supply side effects will create the capacity for higher output and the incentives for higher work effort. However, capacity creating investment is not planned, financed, and constructed overnight; it takes years. But the demand side effects of a tax cut are immediate, reaching full effect within a few calendar quarters. Therefore, the effects of a substantial tax cut enacted when excess capacity is low, based on Laffer-type faith, would be a rapid increase in demand, which would quickly accelerate price increases and raise interest rates, thus choking off the hoped for increase in investment.

5. Professor Laffer and the adherents to his concepts claim that the United States is presently in the "prohibitive range" of the Laffer Curve, i.e. that the "tax rate" is so high and stifling of incentives that an across-the-board tax cut would actually increase revenues rather than reduce them. However, there is virtually no evidence to support this assertion. If this assertion were true one would expect effective tax rates to have risen dramatically in the U.S. in recent years; however Federal taxes as a percentage of CNR or personal income have remained virtually constant over the last quarter century.[6] If this assertion were true one might also expect to find that the U.S. tax burden considerably exceeds that of the other developed countries of the World; however, total taxes in the U.S. as a percent of GNP are lower than the average for the OECD countries. Some countries which have higher productivity growth than the U.S., for example Germany and Sweden, also have higher overall tax burdens.

For a tax cut to be self-financing, its impact on the economy would have to be so large that the new tax revenue generated would more than compensate for the original revenue loss. Total Federal taxes in the U.S. claim roughly 20 percent of GNP. Thus, for a tax cut to increase Federal revenues, rather than add to the deficit, it would have to increase GNP by a multiple of 5 times its original size or more. No analysis of fiscal policy in the U.S. economy has concluded that such a high multiplier for an overall tax cut is possible. The major econometric models of the U.S. economy all have multiplier effects for various fiscal policies which range from about 1.3 to 2. Therefore, a tax cut will reduce tax revenue by about 60 percent to 75 percent of the original amount of the reduction, with the remainder replaced by revenue from the feedback effect.[7]

Thus, despite the other beneficial effects, one inevitable result of a tax cut with undiminished spending is an increase in the deficit.

6. Part of the intuitive appeal of the Laffer Curve derives from the interpretation of point E on the curve. This point is the crossover point to the "prohibitive range" of the Laffer Curve where incentives are so bruised that higher taxes

---

[6]Total Federal, State and local taxes have increased about 2 percent as a portion of GNP over the same era.
[7]The feedback effect on the Federal deficit, as opposed to just tax revenues, is somewhat larger because a more vigorous economy also reduces expenditures, for example welfare and unemployment compensation. However, the effect still falls considerably short of providing a "self-financing" tax cut.

yield lower revenues. It is also claimed to be the point at which the electorate desires to be taxed, in other words, an optimal size for government at which just the right amount of public services is provided. It is an easy deductive leap from the asserted coincidence of these two points to conclude that if government becomes only slightly larger than the electorate would prefer, then we enter the prohibitive range and taxation becomes oppressive.

However, there is no reason to believe that these two points are the same. The desired level of government services in the U.S. is not determined by raising taxes until higher tax rates produce lower revenues; if so tax rates would undoubtedly be much higher than presently. The desired level of government in this country is determined through the political process, and there is nothing which suggests that the size of government produced by that process is the maximum possible which can be imposed without suppressing productive enterprise. In fact, the overwhelming evidence is to the contrary. In the United States the determinants of the optimal size of government have more to do with the desire for personal freedom and a preference for private production of goods and services than with diminishing returns from higher levels of taxation. Thus, the optimal size of government in this country is probably very small compared to point E on the Laffer Curve, and the relatively small variations in government size around the optimal point which result from the political decision making process do not currently appear to run the risk of entering the "prohibitive range" of taxation on the Laffer Curve.

7. The Kemp/Roth advocates have contributed an important observation regarding the effect of taxation on incentives. Recently, considerable attention has been focused from many quarters on the effect of taxation on capital formation and incentives to invest. However, the Kemp/Roth proponents have added to this discussion the observation that the individual income tax has become more of a general economic disincentive over the past 13 years because taxpayers have been pushed into increasingly higher marginal tax brackets.

As a general principle, a tax with lower marginal tax rates is less destructive of economic incentives, and therefore more efficient in an overall economic sense (i.e. it imposes less of a cost on society as a whole), than a tax with higher marginal tax rates. Of course, two equal-revenue income taxes with different marginal tax rate schedules will not be exact substitutes because they will not distribute the tax burden in precisely the same manner; the tax with the lower marginal rates will require a larger tax base, either by virtue of having a smaller standard deduction and personal exemptions, or by having a broader tax base with fewer or smaller itemized deductions and exclusions.[8]

However, it is possible to design an income tax with somewhat lower marginal tax rates and only a moderately larger tax base. Specifically, when a tax cut is being considered for fiscal policy reasons, the tax cut can be accomplished by lowering the tax rates, or by increasing the size of the standard deduction, personal exemptions, or general tax credit. Depending on which mechanism is chosen, the distribution of the overall tax burden after the tax cut will be somewhat different, but not greatly so (obviously depending on the size of the tax

---

[8]For example see: Department of the Treasury, Blueprints for Basic Tax Reform, January 17, 1977, 230 p. for the presentation of a comprehensive income tax with a substantially broader tax base and a three-bracket rate schedule with marginal rates of 8, 25, and 38 percent.

TABLE 1
Tax Returns Classified by Highest Marginal Rate
at Which Tax Was Computed, 1965 and 1975

	Percent of Taxable Returns Classified by Highest Marginal Rate at Which Tax Was Computed			
	1965		1975	
Tax Bracket (marginal tax rates)	Percent of Taxable Returns	Cumulative Percent	Percent of Taxable Returns	Cumulative Percent
14 percent	12.3	12.3	6.6	6.6
15 percent	11.2	23.5	5.2	11.9
16 percent	11.7	35.2	6.1	17.9
17 to 18 percent	12.6	47.8	6.7	34.6
19 to 20 percent	33.4	81.2	22.2	46.8
21 to 24 percent	11.9	93.1	24.2	71.0
25 to 29 percent	4.9	98.0	20.3	91.3
30 to 39 percent	1.0	99.0	6.3	97.6
40 to 49 percent	.38	99.4	1.3	98.9
50 to 59 percent	.46	99.9	.9	99.8
60 to 70 percent	.06	99.9	.3	100.0

Note: The data in the table are for returns with taxable income; these returns as a percent of total tax returns and in comparison to total population have remained fairly constant between 1965 and 1975.

Source: Author's calculations based on data in Internal Revenue Service, Department of the Treasury, Statistics of Income, Individual Income Tax Returns, for years 1965, 1975.

cut).[9] Over a lengthy period of time, as inflation and increases in real income push taxpayers into ever higher tax brackets, the choice of tax cut mechanism can make a substantial difference in the distribution of the tax burden and in the marginal tax rates faced by taxpayers.

The last tax cut in the United States which was achieved by reducing the marginal tax rates was the 1964 tax cut.[10] In the intervening years there have been several tax reductions affecting the individual income tax (in 1969, 1971, 1975, 1976, and 1977), but all have been accomplished by increasing the standard deduction or the personal exemption, or by creating new devices such as the general tax credit or the low income allowance.

However, these changes have not been sufficient to prevent a general movement of taxpayers into higher tax brackets, and since the tax rates have remained constant, the marginal rates experienced by many taxpayers have increased. This phenomenon is documented in Table 1 which classifies tax returns by tax bracket for 1965 (the year the 1964 tax cut became fully effective) and 1975 (the last year for which data are available). . . . As the table and figure reveal, there has been a clear and substantial upward movement of taxpayers into higher marginal tax rate brackets (the movement would be even more

[9]The choice of tax cut mechanism may substantially affect the distribution of the *benefits of the tax cut*, but not significantly affect the distribution of the *overall tax burden* after the tax cut.
[10]This statement ignores the reduction in tax rates which occurred when the surtax expired in 1970.

substantial by 1978). For example, in 1965 only 19 percent of taxpayers faced a marginal tax rate higher than 20 percent, and only 7 percent had marginal rates of 25 percent or higher; in 1975 these percentages were 53 percent and 29 respectively.[11] This implies that substantially larger numbers of taxpayers are now in the upper rate brackets in which the marginal tax rate may begin to erode economic incentives. In this regard it is significant that both the Kemp/Roth bill and the 1978 tax cut proposal by President Carter would reduce taxes by an across-the-board reduction in tax rates rather than by further changes in the standard deduction or personal exemption.

A SUMMARY OF THE ECONOMETRIC ANALYSES
OF THE KEMP/ROTH TAX CUT BILL

This section summarizes the results of three studies of the prospective economic impact of the Kemp/Roth bill using the econometric models of Data Resources, Inc.,[12] Wharton Forecasting Associates, Inc.,[13] and Chase Econometric Associates, Inc.[14] The DRI and Wharton simulations were performed by the Congressional Research Service; the Chase analysis was conducted by Chase Econometric Associates for Congressman Kemp and Senator Roth.[15]

To some extent the results of the studies are a lesson in the uncertainties of using the econometric models as much as they are indications of the prospective economic impacts of the Kemp/Roth bill.

The results of the three studies differ, in some instances substantially, for several reasons. First, the results of each study are obviously dependent on the structure of the econometric model employed; because the models differ, the results will also differ. This problem is intensified by the magnitude of the Kemp/Roth tax cut. The econometric models all produce somewhat similar results for moderate changes in policy and short-term projections.

However, they are not especially well suited for analyzing the implications of dramatic policy changes, especially over long time periods. Sizeable policy shifts may push models into unrealistic ranges where their structural differences are significant; for example the models differ in their response to policies that would reduce unemployment to unrealistically low levels. Second, the models produce different forecasts of the path of the economy in the absence of a tax cut. Since the impact of a tax cut is dependent on the state of the economy,

---

[11]A second result of cutting taxes by means other than rate reductions over the past 15 years is that the tax burden has shifted among income classes with the lower-income groups benefitting and middle-and-upper-income groups suffering higher effective tax rates. See Sunley, Emil M., and Joseph A. Pechman, "Inflation Adjustments for the Individual Income Tax," in *Inflation and the Income Tax*, Henry Aaron, Ed., The Brookings Institution, Washington, D.C., 1976. p. 160.

[12]Amerkhail, Valerie Lowe, "Analysis of the Economic Impact of H.R. 8333," Economics Division, Congressional Research Service, Library of Congress, March 22, 1978. 11 p.

[13]Amerkhail, Valerie Lowe, "Analysis of the Economic Impact of H.R. 8333, Using the Wharton Annual Model," Economics Division, Congressional Research Service, Library of Congress, June 27, 1978. 8 p.

[14]Computer Printouts dated March 30, 1978: provided by the office of the Honorable Jack Kemp.

[15]Chase now has two other versions of the analysis of the Kemp/Roth bill, one incorporating a larger cut in Government spending and the other adding a larger corporate tax cut. See Evans, Michael K., Statement at Hearing on Kemp/Roth Tax Cut Bills, Subcommittee on Taxation and Debt Management, Senate Finance Committee, July 14, 1978. For an analysis of these Chase studies see Amerkhail, Valerie Lowe, "Simulations of the Economic Impact of the Kemp/Roth Tax Cut Proposals by Chase Econometrics," Economics Division, Congressional Research Service, Library of Congress, Forthcoming.

the models will obviously yield different impact estimates if they project different growth paths (e.g., a "growth recession" versus continued moderate growth). Third, the assumptions employed in the analyses differ.

The assumed size of the Kemp/Roth tax cut in the DRJ and Wharton studies is the same as indicated in section I of this paper; however, the size of the tax cut in the Chase simulations is much smaller, rising to only 20 percent in the third year rather than 33 percent.[16] Additionally, the Chase simulation implicitly reduces real Government spending as the tax cut is phased in because in the Chase model nominal Government expenditures are held constant rather than real spending.

The results reported below compare the projected economic impact of the Kemp/Roth tax cut to economic projections assuming no tax cut in 1978–79 and to alternative projections assuming adoption of a moderate tax cut in 1978 resulting from President Carter's proposals in January. In addition to other differences in the assumptions, the comparative simulations also assume different sizes for the Carter tax cut. The DRI simulation assumes a Carter tax cut of $13.3 billion in the individual income tax plus a reduction of the corporate tax rate to 46 percent and an increase in the effective rate of the investment tax credit from 9 percent to 12.5 percent. The Wharton simulation assumes an aggregate tax cut to $26 billion affecting individual and corporate income taxes. The Chase projection assumes a $32 billion aggregate tax cut.[17]

Gross National Product

Table 2 displays the results of the econometric simulations regarding levels of real GNP and the growth rate of real GNP. Generally, the results imply that the Kemp/Roth bill would have a sizeable positive impact on real GNP which would peak in the early 1980's and dissipate by the late 1980's. The Wharton simulation shows a more lasting impact of the tax cut on real GNP, but all of the projections show the increase in the real GNP growth rate disappearing or turning negative by 1987. The Chase impact estimates are smaller than the others because the Chase simulated tax cut is smaller and is accompanied by a reduction in real Government spending.

Unemployment Rate and Employment

Table 3 reports the output of the simulations regarding the unemployment rate and the total level of employment. Again, the results generally imply a substantial favorable impact of the Kemp/Roth bill which would peak in the early 1980's and dissipate in the later 1980's. The Wharton simulation shows a more sizeable lasting effect on the unemployment rate (total employment was not simulated in the Wharton Study) and the Chase impact estimates are somewhat smaller than the other two.

Special caution must be exercised in interpreting these employment projections. Both the DRI and Wharton projections imply overall unemployment rates

---

[16]The assumed tax cuts in the Chase simulations are 6.9 percent the first year, 13.2 percent the second year and 20.1 percent the third year. See Amerkhail, "Simulations of the Economic Impact of the Kemp/Roth Tax Cut Proposals by Chase Econometrics," op. cit.

[17]The reason for the differing versions of the Carter tax cut is these forecasts were taken from the standard forecast of each econometric service at the time of the analysis.

TABLE 2
Projected Impact of Kemp/Roth Tax Cut Bill
on Real GNP and Real GNP Growth Rate, 1978–87

	1978	1979	1980	1982	1987
Percent change in real GNP (1972 dollars):					
Compared to no tax cut:					
DRI	1.1	2.8	4.9	6.0	0.2
Wharton	1.5	2.9	4.8	6.0	7.1
Chase	.4	1.2	2.4	2.7	1.5
Compared to Carter tax cut:					
DRI	.9	2.1	3.9	5.3	−.5
Wharton	.9	2.4	3.9	4.0	3.4
Chase	.2	.1	0	.5	−.4
Percentage point change in growth rate of real GNP:					
Compared to no tax cut:					
DRI	1.2	1.7	2.1	.1	.7
Wharton	1.5	1.5	1.8	.8	−.1
Chase	.4	.9	1.2	−.3	.0
Compared to Carter tax cut:					
DRI	1.0	1.2	1.8	.3	−.7
Wharton	.9	1.6	1.5	.2	−.4
Chase	.3	−.1	−.1	.3	0

below 4 percent in the 1980's, with the rate in the Wharton projection reaching a low of 2.1 percent. Most economists would argue that there is some minimal level of structural unemployment[18] which cannot be further reduced by fiscal policy measures. The actual unemployment level associated with this "full employment" condition is the subject of some debate, but it is widely regarded to be between 4.5 and 5.5 percent. The econometric models do not have structural characteristics which prevent them from projecting unemployment rates below this range. Therefore, results such as those in the table would normally call for external adjustments of the simulations to produce more realistic forecasts. Since the purpose of these analyses was not an actual forecast, but rather a comparative impact simulation, such external adjustments were not made. However, it is important in interpreting the results to note that the impact of the Kemp/Roth bill on employment and unemployment would most likely be smaller than shown in Table 3, and consequently the impact on inflation would probably be larger.

Inflation

Table 4 shows the econometric projections of the impact of the Kemp/Roth tax cut on the consumer price index. In general, the results imply that the proposal would gradually increase the inflation rate with a substantial acceler-

[18]Structural unemployment generally refers to unemployment associated with skill level or locational problems rather than insufficient aggregate demand.

TABLE 3
Projected Impact of Kemp/Roth Bill on Unemployment Rate and Employment, 1978–87

	1978	1979	1980	1982	1987
Percentage point change in unemployment rate:					
Compared to no tax cut:					
DRI	−0.3	−1.0	−1.7	−2.3	−0.1
Wharton	−.5	−1.1	−2.1	−3.3	−4.0
Chase	−.1	−.6	−.3	−1.7	−.9
Compared to Carter tax cut:					
DRI	−.3	−.7	−1.3	−2.0	.1
Wharton	−.3	−.9	−1.7	−2.4	−1.9
Chase	−.2	−.2	−.2	−.7	0
Change in employment (millions of persons):					
Compared to no tax cut:					
DRI	.3	1.1	2.0	3.3	.3
Chase	.2	.7	1.4	2.2	1.1
Compared to Carter tax cut:					
DRI	.3	.9	1.7	2.9	−.2
Chase	.5	.5	.5	1.0	.2

TABLE 4
Projected Impact of Kemp/Roth Bill on Consumer Price Index (CPI)
and Annual Rate of Increase in CPI, 1978–87

	1978	1979	1980	1982	1987
Percent change in Consumer Price Index (CPI):					
Compared to no tax cut:					
DRI	0	0.3	0.8	3.6	13.3
Wharton	−.2	−.4	−.4	1.1	10.4
Chase	0	0	.3	1.8	6.8
Compared to Carter tax cut:					
DRI	0	.2	.6	3.1	12.1
Wharton	−.1	−.3	−.2	1.4	10.7
Chase	.1	.3	.6	1.2	3.3
Percentage point change in annual rate of increase in CPI:					
Compared to no tax cut:					
DRI	0	.3	.6	1.8	1.6
Wharton	−.2	−.2	0	1.0	1.7
Chase	0	0	.2	1.0	.7
Compared to Carter tax cut:					
DRI	0	.2	.5	1.6	1.5
Wharton	−.1	−.2	.1	1.1	1.6
Chase	.1	.2	.4	.3	.2

ation by the mid 1980's; by 1987 prices would be at least 10 percent higher, and the annual rate of inflation would be in excess of 1.5 percentage points higher than without the Kemp/Roth tax cut. The Wharton results indicate that the inflation rate would decline somewhat in the early years of the simulation but accelerate thereafter. The Chase simulation shows a smaller inflation impact due to the smaller assumed tax cut and the implicit reduction in the level of real Government spending. Once again, it should be emphasized that the inflation impact estimates are likely considerably understated because the substantially higher levels of aggregate demand and production caused by the Kemp/Roth tax cut would push the economy beyond a condition of full employment early in the 1980's, and this condition is not fully reflected in the estimates.

Interest Rates

Table 5 reports the results of the econometric simulations regarding two selected interest rates: the rate on AA-rated utility bonds and the rate on commercial paper. These interest rates, and others faced by business and consumers, are important determinants of levels of capital investment and consumption. The results imply that the Kemp/Roth bill would cause a gradual increase in interest rates over the next decade, and that by 1987 interest rates would most likely be 1¼ to 2 percentage points higher than otherwise.

Disposable Personal Income and the Savings Rate

Estimates of the impact of the Kemp/Roth bill on real disposable personal income and the rate of savings are displayed in Table 6. The DRI and Chase projections show a significant positive impact on real disposable personal income which peaks in the early 1980's and has diminished considerably by 1987; the Wharton estimates indicate a continuing increase throughout the period. All

TABLE 5
Projected Impact of Kemp/Roth Tax Cut Bill on Interest Rates, 1978–87

	1978	1979	1980	1982	1987
Change in interest rate on AA-rated utility bonds (in basis points):					
Compared to no tax cut:					
DRI	−12	2	31	175	228
Chase	4	17	42	113	116
Compared to Carter tax cut:					
DRI	−9	−4	8	134	192
Chase	−3	7	19	40	34
Changes in interest rates on commercial paper (in basis points):					
Compared to no tax cut:					
Wharton	5	27	50	92	176
Chase	15	50	102	188	128
Compared to Carter tax cut:					
Wharton	3	19	43	73	136
Chase	−1	17	43	81	79

of the models project a sizeable increase in the savings rate peaking in the early 1980's. It should be noted that the savings rate increases projected in the models do not result from enhanced savings incentives caused by lower tax rates as discussed in the previous section. Savings in the models is a residual from disposable personal income and consumption. In the projections saving increases as a percent of income, because marginal consumption as a percent of marginal income is lower than total consumption as a percent of total income. To the extent that savings incentives would increase due to the lower marginal tax rates, the effect on the savings rate could be greater than shown in the estimates; on the other hand, to the extent that the models have overestimated the impact of the Kemp/Roth bill on the unemployment rate and underesti mated the impact on inflation, the savings rate effect could be smaller.

Investment

Table 7 shows projections of the impact of the Kemp/Roth bill on real nonresidential and residential investment; the models produce substantially different results for these variables. Compared to no tax cut the models all show the bill having a sizeable positive impact on real fixed nonresidential investment; DRI and Chase show the impact diminishing by the late 1980's, Wharton shows the effect continuing. Compared to the Carter tax cut, however, all three models show the Kemp/Roth bill having a negative impact on nonresidential investment by 1987; the DRI and Wharton simulations show a positive impact through the early 1980's; the Chase projection shows a minimal impact throughout the period.

TABLE 6
Projected Impact of Kemp/Roth Tax Cut Bill
on Real Disposable Personal Income and the Savings Rate, 1978–87

	1978	1979	1980	1982	1987
Percent change in real disposable personal income:					
Compared to no tax cut:					
DRI	2.1	4.7	7.6	9.1	4.4
Wharton	2.6	5.1	8.3	10.7	15.8
Chase	1.1	2.7	4.6	5.9	5.2
Compared to Carter tax cut:					
DRI	1.8	3.9	6.9	8.6	3.9
Wharton	1.5	4.2	7.0	7.5	10.1
Chase	.8	.6	1.4	1.9	1.1
Percentage point change in savings rate:					
Compared to no tax cut:					
DRI	.7	1.1	1.4	.8	.3
Wharton	.8	1.3	1.7	1.3	1.4
Chase	.6	1.1	1.8	1.8	1.7
Compared to Carter tax cut:					
DRI	.5	1.0	1.4	.8	.5
Wharton	.5	1.1	1.5	.7	.9
Chase	.4	.2	.6	.6	.4

THE LAFFER CURVE

TABLE 7
Projected Impact of Kemp/Roth Tax Cut Bill
on Real Nonresidential and Residential Investment, 1978–87

	1978	1979	1980	1982	1987
Percent change in real fixed nonresidential investment:					
Compared to no tax cut:					
DRI	1.4	4.8	9.5	15.7	−6.5
Wharton	2.5	5.0	8.0	10.2	10.6
Chase	.5	2.4	5.7	8.8	4.9
Compared to Carter tax cut:					
DRI	1.2	2.3	3.9	7.8	−10.4
Wharton	1.3	3.5	5.5	4.3	−2.4
Chase	.1	−.2	−1.3	.7	−2.5
Percent change in real investment in residential structures:					
Compared to no tax cut:					
DRI	1.8	4.2	5.0	−4.7	−23.2
Wharton	4.4	6.2	5.9	3.0	15.2
Chase	.9	2.5	3.2	−1.9	0
Compared to Carter tax cut:					
DRI	1.2	2.9	3.8	−.9	−23.8
Wharton	2.6	5.6	5.1	.5	13.9
Chase	−1.4	.9	1.7	1.2	−.4

The three models differ the most with regard to the impact of the bill on investment in residential structures (this component of investment is notoriously difficult to forecast). The DRI simulation shows a moderate positive impact in the first few years which turns strongly negative in the 1980's. The Wharton projection shows a positive cyclical impact, rising above trend in the first few years, weakening in the early 1980's, and strengthening substantially in the late 1980's. The Chase simulation shows comparatively little impact throughout the period.

The Federal Deficit

Estimates of the impact of the Kemp/Roth bill on the Federal deficit are shown in Table 8. While the magnitudes differ (the Chase estimates are substantially lower than those of DRI and Wharton because of the smaller tax cut simulated by Chase and the implicit reduction in real Government expenditures) one message is clear: the Kemp/Roth bill would substantially increase the Federal deficit over the foreseeable future. The econometric models imply that the tax cut would fall considerably short of "paying for itself," whatever its other benefits may be.

Some proponents of the Kemp/Roth bill have argued that the econometric simulations show that the tax cut would finance itself in a different sense, not that the deficit would decrease or disappear, but rather that any increase in the Federal deficit will be financed by the additional private savings and retained earnings generated by the tax cut. However, this is not a surprising result to

TABLE 8
Projected Impact of Kemp/Roth Tax Cut Bill on the Federal Deficit, 1978–87

	1978	1979	1980	1982	1987
Difference in Federal deficit (billions of dollars):					
Compared to no tax cut:					
DRI	21.1	36.9	54.4	68.5	241.2
Wharton	19.8	40.5	68.4	88.0	158.1
Chase	12.4	24.9	37.9	32.8	36.8
Compared to Carter tax cut:					
DRI	15.1	30.2	56.1	64.9	217.4
Wharton	11.6	32.7	50.5	58.3	104.7
Chase	7.6	3.2	19.8	19.6	41.0

observe from the econometric models because in the models, as in the economy, the deficit will always be financed. The issue is not whether the deficit will be financed, but at what cost in terms of interest rates and inflation, and their further impact on investment and other economic variables.

In summary, the econometric studies of the Kemp/Roth tax cut bill generally imply that bill would have a favorable impact on levels of gross national product, employment, income, savings, and investment; these favorable impacts for the most part would decline, or in some cases reverse, by the mid-to-late 1980's. Additionally, these favorable effects would be accompanied by substantially higher inflation, higher interest rates and a larger Federal deficit.

Vanik's Study Makes Convincing Case for Enactment of the Kemp-Roth Act

JACK KEMP

Congressman Jack Kemp of New York, co-author of the Kemp-Roth tax cut bill, responds to the Library of Congress study's criticism of the bill, focusing particular attention on the findings of the three econometric studies included in the report.

The SPEAKER pro tempore. Under a previous order of the House, the gentleman from New York (Mr. KEMP) is recognized for 15 minutes.

• Mr. KEMP. Mr. Speaker, yesterday afternoon, our colleague from Ohio (Mr. VANIK) read into the RECORD an extensive study prepared at his request by the Library of Congress. He is one of the most articulate spokesmen in Congress against the Kemp-Roth legislation to reduce individual income tax rates. He is a spirited opponent, and as always I welcome the debate which he and I have helped heighten on this crucially important public policy question. Its outcome will substantially affect the future of our economy.

I take this opportunity to thank him for having had a specialist in taxation and fiscal policy at the Library of Congress prepare this study and for bringing it to our attention yesterday.

I thank him because this study helps build the case for the enactment of the Kemp-Roth legislation, for reducing individual income tax rates, for that is the amendment which I intend to offer to the tax bill, H.R. 13511, ordered reported by the Committee on Ways and Means. It makes a very strong case for enactment for the Kemp-Roth measure.

This is truly one of the most remarkable studies and record precedes that I have ever read. Our colleague's rhetoric says the study shows that Kemp-Roth ought not to be enacted. The study's rhetoric says essentially the same thing, particularly in its attack on the premises on which Kemp-Roth rests, although I must say it "hedges its bet" in a number of instances.

Yet the figures which it reports and thereby brings to this debate add substantially to the case for enactment of Kemp-Roth. As a matter of fact, the study brings information to us in support of Kemp-Roth which has never before been made public.

What have VANIK and the Library study helped me show will happen if Kemp-Roth is enacted?

That all categories of taxpayers will have less tax liability.

That the upper income brackets will pay a greater percentage of the total individual income taxes paid to the Federal Government.

Jack Kemp, "Vanik's Library of Congress Study Makes Convincing Case for Enactment of the Kemp-Roth Tax Rate Reduction Act," *Congressional Record*, August 3, 1978, pp. H7858–H7861.

That the real gross national product will increase over what would other-wise occur.

That unemployment would drop dramatically.

That millions of new jobs would be created.

That disposable personal income would rise dramatically.

That the savings rate would increase.

That residential investment would increase and construction accelerate.

That nonresidential investment would increase and construction grow.

That he has not answered satisfactorily his assertion that Kemp-Roth is going to produce monstrous deficits and horrendous inflation.

Let me give specific examples of how this study builds the case for Kemp-Roth.

ALL CATEGORIES OF TAXPAYERS WILL HAVE LESS TAX LIABILITY

All categories of taxpayers will have less tax liability if Kemp-Roth is enacted. They will have to give up less of their income to the Federal Government in the form of taxes. . . .

UPPER INCOME BRACKETS WILL PAY
GREATER PERCENTAGE OF TOTAL TAXES

Income tax liability distribution is offered in such a way that those making less than $30,000 will be paying less of the total individual income taxes paid to Uncle Sam, while those making $30,000 or more will be paying a greater percentage of that total.

Those making between $30,000 and $50,000 are now paying 21.29 percent of the total taxes paid to Washington; that will increase to 21.3 percent. Those making between $50,000 and $100,000 are now paying 13.02 percent of that total; that will increase to 13.2 percent. Then we start to get some big jumps. Those making between $100,000 and $200,000 are now paying 7.12 percent of the total; that will jump to 7.6 percent. And those now making over $200,000, who are now paying 7.45 percent of the total, will be paying 8.5 percent. . . .

FEDERAL INCOME TAX LIABILITY
FOR EVERY CATEGORY OF TAXPAYER REDUCED

The Kemp-Roth bill, or amendment to H.R. 13511, will reduce the Federal income tax liability for every category of taxpayer: single persons, married couples without dependents, married couples with dependents. . . . surviving spouses, heads of households, estates and trusts would also have reduced Federal income tax liability.

REAL GROSS NATIONAL PRODUCT AND
REAL GNP GROWTH RATE WOULD INCREASE

The projected impact of Kemp-Roth on the real gross national product and on the real gross national product growth rate, both discounted for the inflation caused increases in GNP and GNP growth rates, is very favorable.

All three econometric studies used by, and cited in, the Library's study—
Data Resources, Inc. (DRI), Wharton, and Chase Econometrics—show significant increases in real GNP and in real GNP growth rate, compared to no tax cut
and compared to the administration's proposed tax cut. I repeat, all three
econometric studies show this.

Chase says that real GNP would go up 1.2 percent in 1979, if Kemp-Roth
becomes law, compared to no tax cut. Wharton says it would go up to 2.9
percent in that year, and DRI says it would go up 2.8 percent.

Chase says that real GNP would go up 2.4 percent in 1980, if Kemp-Roth
passes, compared to no tax cut. Wharton says it would go up 4.8 percent, and
DRI says it would go up 4.9.

Chase says that it would go up, compared to no tax cut, by 2.7 percent
by 1982. But both Wharton and DRI agree the increase would be 6 percent
that year.

The studies show increases, over what would otherwise occur, in the real
growth rate, discounted for inflation, of real GNP. Chase says 0.9 percent in
1979. Wharton concludes 1.5 percent, and DRI says 1.7 percent. In 1980, Chase
says it would be 1.2 percent higher than what we could otherwise expect; Wharton says 1.8 percent; and DRI concludes 2.1 percent.

Comparisons drawn between Kemp-Roth and the administration's proposed tax cut show similar increases in real GNP and in real GNP growth rates if
Kemp-Roth is enacted over what would occur if the President's proposal were
enacted. This is important because none of the alternatives to Kemp-Roth—the
Vanik-Pickle amendment, the Corman amendment, the Fisher amendment—are
as large as the President's original proposal. Thus, Kemp-Roth would compare
more favorably against them, too.

These figures are drawn from table 1 of the Library's study.

KEMP-ROTH WOULD DROP UNEMPLOYMENT RATE

The Vanik-Library study concludes that the enactment of Kemp-Roth would
substantially reduce unemployment in the United States. Few things could be
more important to the well-being of our people, all of them.

Chase shows the unemployment rate would drop, if Kemp-Roth were
enacted, by 0.6 percent in 1979, but DRI concludes it would drop by a full
percentage point and Wharton concludes it would drop by 1.1 percent.

Chase shows the unemployment rate would drop by 0.3 percent in 1980, but
DRI shows a drop of 1.7 percent and Wharton shows a drop of 2.1 percent.

Chase shows a drop of 0.7 percent in 1982, but DRI shows a dramatic drop
of 2.3 percent and Wharton a staggering 3.3 percent reduction.

When the figures are forecast out to 1987, Wharton shows a drop of a full
4 percentage points.

These figures are drawn from table 3.

KEMP-ROTH WOULD CREATE MILLIONS OF NEW JOBS

The Vanik-Library study then translates these reductions in the unemployment
rates arising from enactment of Kemp-Roth into the number of jobs which
would be created.

Wharton, for some reason, either did not forecast this or the Library decided not to use them, but Chase shows 700,000 new jobs in 1979, with DRI showing 1,100,000 new jobs that year. For 1980, Chase shows 1,400,000, and DRI shows 2 million. For 1982, Chase shows 2.2 million, with DRI showing 3.3 million. The reference here is to table 3 also.

This gives our country massive employment, instead of massive unemployment.

DISPOSABLE PERSONAL INCOME WILL RISE DRAMATICALLY

Chase, Wharton, and DRI all show dramatic increases in real disposable personal income. Real disposable personal income is that income over and above inflation-caused increases. It is real disposable personal income that gives a taxpayer, a family, more purchasing power, a higher living standard.

If Kemp-Roth is enacted, in 1979 Chase says real disposable personal income will go up by 2.7 percent. DRI says 4.7 percent, and Wharton says 5.1 percent.

In 1980, Chase says it would go up 4.6 percent, DRI says 7.6 percent, and Wharton says 8.3 percent.

By 1982, Chase says real disposable personal income that year would climb 5.9 percent, with DRI saying 9.1 percent and Wharton saying 10.7 percent.

The figures are astounding when you stretch the effects of the Kemp-Roth tax rate reductions on the living standard of the people out almost a full decade. Wharton forecasts an increase in 1987 of 15.8 percent.

There are similar figures for comparisons between Kemp-Roth and the administration's proposals. Please see table 6.

THE SAVINGS RATE WOULD INCREASE UNDER KEMP-ROTH

People would save more of their income, if Kemp-Roth were enacted. That is the conclusion of all three econometric models. I think savings would go up even higher than the figures projected here, and I have addressed myself to this point in floor remarks in the past several weeks: July 14, H6783–H6789; July 26, H7397–H7400; and August 1, H7672–H7674. I invite all my colleagues to read carefully the savings questions raised and answered in those three pieces, because they relate not only to the savings question but also to the Federal deficits and inflation potential questions.

That notwithstanding, all three models do predict increases in the savings rate. Chase says savings would go up by 1.1 percent in 1979; DRI agrees, but Wharton says 1.3 percent. DRI says 1.4 percent, Wharton 1.7 percent, and Chase 1.8 percent in 1980. There are similar projections for later years and in contrast with the administration's bill.

I find it very interesting that this table, table 6, gives us no definition of savings. If savings is aggregate personal savings, aggregate retained earnings of corporations, and investment assets, that is one thing. If it is just aggregate personal savings, that is another. The reason this is important is that increases in personal savings and retained earnings are what will offset the potential net deficits, after feedback from an expanded economic base, and thereby mean little or no inflation. Inflation is a product of Government expanding the money supply, which it has done in order to pay part of Federal deficits. If there is a sufficient increase in savings and retained earnings to cover that deficit, then there will be no need for creating additional money, thus no inflation from that, and there will be no crowding out of investment capital. As a matter of fact, if savings respond the way we think they will and have articulated in the three RECORDS references I have just cited, we will have crowding in. Table 8 is essentially irrelevant to this House's deliberations until that and related questions are answered, for we do not know the premises for which the conclusions were drawn in table 8.

RESIDENTIAL AND NON-RESIDENTIAL CONSTRUCTION WOULD INCREASE

The enactment of Kemp-Roth would be a dramatic spur to residential investment and nonresidential investment, thus to residential construction and nonresidential construction. Employment in the severely depressed building trades would increase commensurately; millions in the building trades now out of work or underemployed would return and be fully employed. No doubt, this is a major part of the increases in jobs and decreases in unemployment reflected in other tables.

Chase says real fixed nonresidential investment would go up by 2.4 percent in 1979, if Kemp-Roth is passed. DRI says 4.8 percent and Wharton says 5 percent.

Chase says 5.7 percent in 1980, Wharton says 8.0 percent and DRI says 9.5 percent.

In 1982, Chase says it will rise by 8.8 percent. Wharton says 10.2 percent and DRI says a staggering 15.7 percent.

The figures are in the same pattern for additional investment in residential structures.

Chase shows a percentage increase of 2.5 in 1979, DRI shows 4.2, and Wharton says 6.2. In 1980 Chase says we would have a 3.2 percent increase, DRI says 5 percent and Wharton says 5.9 percent.

These figures are drawn from table 7.

VANIK-LIBRARY STUDY CONFUSES DEFICIT AND INFLATION QUESTIONS, DOES NOT ANSWER THEM

Our colleague's assertion, that of Walter Heller, that of our colleague from Connecticut (Mr. GIAIMO) and that of the CBO study which he released, that Kemp-Roth will increase the deficit to such an extent that inflation will rage across the land, has not been reinforced by this study, as he claims it has in his introduction of it yesterday.

If we are to have such disastrous and disruptive inflation during the period forecast by three econometric studies in the Library's report, then why do we—simultaneously—have an increase in real GNP? An increase in the real GNP growth rate? A drop in unemployment and the creation of jobs for millions? A rise in real disposable personal income? A rise in the savings rate and the amount of real dollars—not inflated dollars—saved by the taxpayers and consumers? A rise in residential investment and construction? A rise in nonresidential investment and construction?

Let me discuss why Kemp-Roth is not inflationary.

WHY KEMP-ROTH IS NOT INFLATIONARY

With so many economic decisions affected by tax rates, it is obvious that the market supply of goods and services must respond to changes in tax rates.

Our economy functions because people respond to changes in relative prices. The price of butter relative to that of margarine. Or beef relative to chicken. Capital relative to labor, and so on.

A tax rate change is just another relative price change. It changes the prices of leisure and current consumption in terms of foregone current and future income.

To claim that people do not respond to these price changes goes against the basic principles of economic science.

Yet there is no recognition of such responses in the economics now used to brand Kemp-Roth, the Tax Rate Reduction Act, as wildly inflationary. This is the charge of our colleague, of a portion of the Library's new study, of Walter Heller.

Walter Heller tells us,* in contrast to what we know about the impact of tax rates on economic decisionmaking, that the decision to save does not depend on the relative prices of current consumption and future income. He tells us that the so-called Denison's Law shows that savings do not respond to higher after-tax reward. The problem here is that Denison's Law is inherent in the formulae structure of almost all of the econometric models. Thus, it skews their calculations on expansion of the tax base, deficits, and inflation.

But the most recent empirical studies of the responsiveness of savings conclude that "private savings is indeed strongly affected by changes in the real after-tax rate of return." As a matter of fact, the principal study dismisses Denison's Law as a "conjecture based on evidence which is flimsy at best and dangerously misleading at worst."

I do not know why Walter Heller is not on top of major studies in and changes going on in the economics profession. Of course, he may have known of the study and its conclusions, but did not want to believe it, refer to it, or incorporate it in his article, or into his own judgment as to the value of Kemp-Roth, for non-economic reasons. After all, he and his career have been closely identified with partisan politics.

But a current understanding of the Kemp-Roth bill's effect on savings is absolutely crucial to assessing an asserted inflationary effect.

Let's try to reach such an understanding. In order to judge the impact of a cut in marginal tax rates on growth and inflation, we have to know what the cut will do to GNP and saving. To finance itself without causing inflation, a tax cut can do four things:

First. It should increase GNP, which is the tax base, and get back revenues to offset some or all of the initial cut.

Second. It should cause existing savings and investment funds to switch out

*Editor's note: For Heller's views, see his article "The Kemp-Roth-Laffer Free Lunch," beginning on page 46.

of tax shelters and nontaxable uses into taxable uses, raising the tax base and revenue. (This probably also raises GNP by shifting saving and investment from low-yield, but sheltered, projects into straightforward, high-yield activities.)

Third. A tax cut should make saving more rewarding after taxes. It should raise the total amount of saving in the economy. Some of this saving would go to buy the bonds the Treasury may have to sell to cover any deficit remaining from the tax cut. Any excess would be used to increase net investment and growth.

Fourth. A tax cut should increase incentives for output and employment.

Roth-Kemp, which is a cut in marginal tax rates, will do all of the above as the Library of Congress study shows it will, because the after-tax reward from working and saving will be enlarged.

As long as revenues rise to offset the tax cut, or as long as savings rise by enough to cover any added debt, the Federal Reserve does not have to buy even one additional Treasury bill, and does not have to add one cent to the money supply.

The Chase Econometrics study presented to the Senate Subcommittee on Taxation and Debt Management on July 14 estimates that personal savings, retained earnings, and other capital inflows will rise enough from the tax-rate reductions found in the Roth-Kemp bill to cover any added deficit and to still leave enough saving left over to increase net investment by well over one-half, delivering an enormous boost to real growth.

Thus, Roth-Kemp is not inflationary. It is self-financing four ways. Dr. Heller has forgotten why inflation occurs, and has no way to distinguish between a tax cut which alters incentives, reduces the use of tax shelters, and stimulates savings and investment, and one which simply cuts Federal revenue and forces the Federal Reserve to create money to buy Treasury debt.

If the Roth-Kemp bill is self-financing, why does Chase predict small increases in inflation rates from Roth-Kemp? Note first, these increases are very small for a tax cut. But, note more importantly, Roth-Kemp does not inherently require the inflationary printing of money to finance it.

THE CASE FOR KEMP-ROTH WELL MADE

Mr. Speaker, as I said at the outset, I want to thank the gentleman from Ohio (Mr. Vanik) for putting this new Library of Congress study into the Record. I do not know why he did so, for when you contrast the rhetoric with the charts, he has given us a contradiction almost without parallel. I can only ask "why?"

But aside from that rhetoric, the study's charts give us the hard statistic data needed to support Kemp-Roth when it comes to the floor. They help make the case for Kemp-Roth.

It is a case well made.

Alms for the Rich

MICHAEL KINSLEY

Attacking the Laffer Curve theory, Michael Kinsley questions the assumption that tax revenues would disappear if tax rates increased to 100 percent and criticizes the lack of evidence indicating whether the current tax rate is actually in the prohibitive range. Of the proposed legislation based on the Laffer theory, Kinsley focuses his discussion on the Steiger-Hansen bill, viewing it as a break for the affluent sector while disguised as part of the middle-class tax revolt.

In 1972 Jude Wanniski went to work as an editorial writer for *The Wall Street Journal*. "Fortunately," Wanniski writes in his recent book, *The Way The World Works* (Basic Books), "I came to the editorial page in 1972 ignorant of all economic dogma." He became interested in taxes; possibly he was paying more of them than he had in the past. At some point Wanniski had a dazzling—one might even say blinding—revelation. It took the form of a conservative paranoid fantasy. What if the government raised taxes to 100 percent and took away every penny people earned? Why, people might not bother to keep working, Wanniski reasoned, and the government—serves it right!—would end up with no money at all. Furthermore, he reasoned backward, the only way the government could get out of this bind and increase its revenues would be by *reducing* taxes.

This insight about high taxes had an effect on Wanniski just the opposite of what his theory suggests. Far from abandoning his labors, he has been reasoning backwards feverishly ever since. One result is *The Way The World Works*. A more astonishing result is the apparently successful effort in Congress to expand the tax loophole for capital gains. Wanniski's editorials in *The Wall Street Journal* implanted the notion that cutting taxes for a tiny minority can benefit everybody and even raise government revenues by unleasing the creative potential of the well-to-do. Placed in today's political soil that is so receptive to reactionary ideas, and fertilized by business propaganda, the seed has flowered. This malignant growth has completely overrun President Carter's own garden of tax reforms, which originally included a proposal to *reduce* the capital gains loophole.

Almost overnight, it seems, a new consensus has emerged about the best way to stimulate the economy. The old view, labeled Keynesian, emphasizes that a tax cut (or a federal budget increase) stimulates aggregate demand by putting more spending money in people's hands. The new conservative theory emphasizes that cutting tax rates can stimulate the *supply* of goods and services by increasing the after-tax return for productive activity. The difference in emphasis is crucial. The Keynesian theory encourages tax cuts aimed primarily at poorer people, who are more likely to spend the extra money right away. The new conservative theory justifies tax cuts primarily for the affluent, since they

Michael Kinsley, "Alms for the Rich," *The New Republic*, vol. 179, August 19, 1978, pp. 19-26. Reprinted by permission of THE NEW REPUBLIC, ©1978, The New Republic, Inc.

are the ones whose productivity is allegedly being smothered by high marginal tax rates.

It is worth a brief look at *The Way The World Works* for insight into the insular world view responsible for the new conservative economic wisdom. Jude Wanniski, economist Arthur Laffer, Representative William Steiger (sponsor of the capital gains amendment) and Representative Jack Kemp (sponsor of another bill to increase government revenues by cutting all income taxes by a third) typify the sort of well-scrubbed, youngish conservative ideologues who are increasingly influential in the political debate. They are not neoconservatives. Their intellectual mentors are old battlers like Irving Kristol, but unlike Kristol — or even Ronald Reagan — their paths to wisdom have been free of detours. They are strangers to doubt. Their cultural backgrounds have given them a narrow perspective on the human condition (and on human motivation), which they have not been moved to transcend. Their intellectual development has consisted of preconceptions borne out in increasingly sophisticated ways.

The Way The World Works reinterprets all of human history on the basis of Wanniski's own experience as a bourgeois family man and *Wall Street Journal* editorial writer. All behavior, Wanniski has concluded, is best understood as a response to tax rates.

> The infant learns, for example, something that politicians and economists frequently forget, which is that there are always two rates of taxation that produce the same revenue. When the infant lies silently and motionless in his crib upon awakening, mother remains in some other room. The "tax rate" on mother is zero, yielding zero attentiveness. On the other hand, when baby screams all the time demanding attention, even when fed and dry, he discovers that mother also remains in the other room and perhaps even closes the nursery door. The tax rate is 100 percent, also yielding zero attentiveness . . . It is always harder to get mother to play when mother is on the telephone than when mother is not. When mother is fixing dinner, it is very difficult to get her to play, but this means father will be home soon and it is usually easy to get him to play . . . By the time children are three or four years old, they have acquired such a body of information by studying tax schedules and their variables within the family that they can consciously "think on the margin."

Wanniski uses his recently acquired tools of economic analysis (to raid his own pantry of domestic imagery) like a child with a new crayon, who marks up all the walls and floors as well as the writing pad it was intended for. Turning his gaze from domestic affairs to the broader historical pageant, Wanniski blames high tax rates for the popularity of socialism, the decline of Hollywood, the existence of prostitution, World War II and the Quebec separatist movement. Low tax rates get credit for events as seemingly unrelated as the rise of Alexander the Great and the US economic boom of the mid-1960s.

The centerpiece of Wanniski's world view is the now-famous "Laffer curve." The British economist A.W.H. Phillips invented his Phillips curve — which purports to measure the trade-off between inflation and unemployment — many years before it became widely known. Arthur B. Laffer of the University of Southern California has achieved this economist's version of immortality only four years after he first drew his curve on a napkin in a Washington restaurant, thanks to skillful promotion by himself, Wanniski, Kemp and other members of the club. Laffer's curve purports to measure the relationship between tax rates and government revenues. It looks like a McDonald's arch, usually turned sideways. A tax rate of zero, Laffer reasons, generates no government revenue. As the tax rate goes up, so do revenues, but not proportionally. This is because taxes create a "wedge" between what the economy is paying for a person's services or the use of his money, and what he is actually getting for them. The wedge is the difference between salary and takehome pay, and the difference between pre-tax and after-tax investment profits. The wedge reduces tax revenues because it discourages the activity — working or investing — that is being taxed. As the wedge gets bigger, people spend more and more of their time and money on untaxed activity. This generally means leisure instead of work, and consumption instead of investment. But untaxed activity also includes endeavors as diverse as growing your own vegetables, expense account lunches, legal tax shelters and illegal tax frauds. All of these become more appealing as tax rates go up.

Eventually, Laffer argues, higher taxes actually reduce government revenues because the effect of the wedge in discouraging taxable activity overwhelms the effect of the higher rate in bringing in more money from the activity that survives. At this point the curve turns back toward zero. When the wedge hits 100 percent, all taxable activity — and thus all tax revenue — stops. The importance of all this is that between these two points it should be possible to *raise* government revenues by *cutting* taxes. This is because reducing the wedge will stimulate new taxable activity, and the revenue from this will more than outweigh the loss from lower rates.

It's easy to see why the Laffer curve has hypnotized conservatives. It suggests that liberals have been so zealous and naive in raising taxes that they have actually lowered the revenues available for their foolish government programs. It also provides a scapegoat for the rather slothful performance of American capitalism over the past few years, and a justification for tax cuts aimed at those in what realtors call "the upper brackets." But there are two problems, one theoretical and one practical, with the Laffer curve and its implied nostrum of lower taxes for the well-off.

The starting point of the Laffer curve — zero taxes, zero government revenues — is a logical necessity. But the end point—100 percent taxes, zero government revenues—exists only for the purpose of argument. It is a theoretical construct, like (say) the square root of minus-one. What would it mean for the government to tax earnings at 100 percent? The Laffer curve assumes that tax revenues simply disappear. If the government imposed a 100 percent tax, then dumped the proceeds in the ocean, people would soon starve, emigrate or revolt, with fatal effect on the tax base. But ordinarily governments spend tax revenues for goods and services they think—however foolishly—will benefit their citizens. A 100 percent tax actually would mean that the government had taken complete control over the distribution of what the economy produced. Perhaps the government would attempt to adopt a system of "from each according to ability, to each according to need." Communist governments may have discouraged productivity, but they have not destroyed it completely. Non-monetary incentives—patriotism, fear, pride, peer pressure—apparently do have some effect. Human motivation is complex (you will be pleased to hear). Even the capitalist elite here in America may not be moved exclusively by financial considerations.

If government revenues wouldn't necessarily drop to zero even at a tax rate of 100 percent, there's no logical reason to assume without proof that the Laffer curve ever reverses direction at all. And if the curve never turns back down, it is not possible to increase revenues by cutting taxes. In real life, of course, the shape of the Laffer curve will be different for every different kind of tax. Whether any particular tax can get so high that it is self-defeating will depend on the type of activity being taxed and the opportunities for evasion.

The practical problem with Laffer's thesis is that even if this backward-turning part of his curve exists, neither he nor any of his supporters has demonstrated that the federal income tax actually is on it. Cutting some taxes to stimulate productivity might be wise policy, but the notion that this can be a free lunch—that taxes can be cut without reducing government revenues—is pure speculation.

The weight of all this theorizing has now settled on the tax rules about capital gains. "It is the bright young college graduate in engineering or physics, or the energetic young entrepreneur, who is chilled by the forbidding rates of capital gains taxation," Wanniski writes. "In 1977, most discussion of capital gains in Congress is in the direction of tightening treatment even further." In 1978 the *only* major tax change likely to pass Congress is a *lowering* of taxes on capital gains, thanks mostly to a brilliant propaganda and lobbying campaign led by Charls Walker, business lobbyist *par excellence* and head of something called the American Council for Capital Formation. You can imagine what this group is, and it is not composed of bright young college graduates and energetic young entrepreneurs. As John Kenneth Galbraith admonished on "Meet the Press" recently, "When people talk about encouraging capital investment, it usually means more income for themselves." But as Charls Walker told *The Washington Post* earlier this month, "In this game, it's the perception that counts." So on behalf of his clients in the upper reaches of corporate capitalism, Walker is invoking the sufferings of the small businessman and the middle-class homeowner. Mobil Corporation and W. R. Grace are buying newspaper ads to join in the chorus. Walker decided on a big capital gains push early this year, and crowned the fortunate, formerly obscure Representative Steiger as his front man.

Despite the talk of "forbidding" capital gains taxes, most references to capital gains in the Internal Revenue Code concern ways in which profits from the sale of capital assets are *not* taxed. Indeed the present capital gains provisions are a layered history of the ebb and flow of favoritism and half-hearted reform. The basic rule is that half of all capital gains each year don't count as taxable income. In effect, this means that capital gains are taxed at half the taxpayer's rate for ordinary income, whatever that rate might be. That was thought to be too harsh on those in high brackets, so Congress created the "alternative tax." This permits the taxpayer to choose a flat 25 percent tax on capital gains. Then Congress decided this was too generous, so it placed a $50,000 annual ceiling on the amount of gains eligible for the alternative tax. It also created a "minimum tax," an especially complicated provision intended to squeeze a bit of money out of people who benefit from large deductions for capital gains and other "preference income." Then there's the capital gains set-off against the "maximum tax," but we won't get into that.

President Carter's original tax package included a proposal to abolish the alternative tax. This would assure that every taxpayer would pay at least half as much tax on capital gains as on ordinary income. The Steiger amendment instead would abolish the *ceiling* on the alternative tax. It also would exempt capital gains from the minimum tax and end the maximum tax set-off. These changes would assure that no individual's capital gain is taxed at more than 25 percent. Steiger's proposal also would reduce the tax on corporate capital gains from 30 percent to 25 percent. This is an important break for businesses like the timber industry which already enjoy special provisions allowing them to treat their profits as capital gains.

Some new special break for capital gains is inevitable. Both houses of Congress are determined to get it and President Carter is resigned. But the final arrangements still were unclear at the end of last week. The House Ways and Means Committee reported out a compromise bill—engineered by Charls Walker and Representative James Jones, but tactfully referred to as the Jones-Ullman Compromise—that would exempt capital gains from the minimum tax, but also abolish the alternative tax. This would mean capital gains would be taxed at exactly half the taxpayer's ordinary rate—up to a maximum of 35 percent. House liberals were hoping to reinstate a new, weaker form of the minimum tax in floor debate.

Any House bill offering less than the full Steiger treatment for capital gains will be in trouble in the Senate. A majority of senators has endorsed the Steiger amendment. Russell Long, Senate Finance Committee chairman, has planned various other amendments that would lighten the load on capital gains even more. There probably will be an effort on the Senate floor to reopen the biggest capital gains loophole of all, which was finally closed last year. This loophole wiped out any capital gains tax due on property that passed at death. The profit on inherited property was measured for tax purposes by its value when inherited, rather than its value when originally purchased. Most capital gains of the very wealthy completely escaped taxation because of the provision. Now that the impact of closing it has begun to sink in, there is pressure to undo that reform as well.

If there ever was special-interest legislation, this capital gains fiddling is it. Think of how much money you'd have to be making before the Steiger amendment would help you. The alternative tax doesn't even apply until you've hit the 50 percent tax bracket, which is $47,200 for a married couple. Before the current $50,000 ceiling (which Steiger would abolish) affects you, you have to have made $97,200 after all other deductions. The minimum tax can affect those with somewhat lower income, but only if most of that income is capital gain.

The propaganda in favor of the Steiger amendment repeatedly claims that capital gains are taxed at rates of up to 50 percent. This is hot air. Because of the tax code's complexity, an effective rate of about 49 percent is possible. But *The Wall Street Journal* itself pointed out recently that someone with $15 million of income, $10 million of it capital gain, would pay only 47 percent. The average tax on capital gain income is about 16 percent. (Marginal rates on ordinary income, by comparison, begin at 14 percent.) Only seven percent of taxpayers with capital gains pay more than 25 percent on any of them. Since less than six percent of all taxpayers have capital gains at all, this means the Steiger amendment would benefit about four taxpayers out of a thousand.

These figures demonstrate the genius of the lobbying campaign that has made the Steiger amendment appear to be part of the revolt of the "average" or "middle-class" taxpayer. Even "the ordinary investor" (Clayton Fritchey's phrase in a recent pro-Steiger column) would not benefit from these proposed changes in the tax code. The only beneficiaries will be those with very large investment profits.

The other major tax change next year, as it happens, will be another Social Security tax hike. The Social Security tax increase is the mirror image of the Steiger tax decrease: it affects *only* ordinary wage income (capital gains, dividends, etc., are exempt), and it places a proportionately greater burden on those with lower wages (because salary income over $17,700 is exempt). (The salaries of congressmen and other federal civilian employees, it should be noted, are totally exempt from the Social Security tax.) The House Ways and Means Committee, while debating the size of the capital gains tax decrease, refused to consider rolling back the scheduled Social Security increase. The Joint Committee on Taxation has computed that because of Social Security and inflation, the current tax "cut" bill actually will guarantee a net tax *increase* next year for practically everybody but the very rich.

An argument heard in favor of the Steiger amendment is that it will prevent the taxation of "illusory" increases in value that are only due to inflation. But of course it will only have this pleasant effect for those with very large capital gains incomes, and it will not distinguish between gains that have occurred quickly and those that have grown over years of inflation. It is true that genuinely middle-class homeowners can be catapulted into a high bracket and socked with a huge tax in the year they sell a house that has appreciated over two or three decades. But the tax code already permits them to escape most of the tax bite if they reinvest in a new house, or if they are over 65. Furthermore, if the time has come to index the tax code for inflation, the profits from home ownership are a bad place to start. The typical homeowner has benefitted from inflation by making his investment with borrowed money, then paying it back over the years in cheaper dollars, while deducting the interest "expense" that may not even have equaled the inflation rate. The tax code is riddled with other special breaks for homeowners, which renters (usually poorer) are not eligible for. (Nevertheless, a bigger capital gains break for homeowners is part of every version of the tax bill, including President Carter's.)

The basic argument for the Steiger amendment is based on the Laffer curve: this tax cut for affluent investors will stimulate the economy, and the benefits will "trickle down" to the rest of us. The stimulus will be so great, America's productive capacity will increase so sharply, that tax revenues will actually increase.

In support of these assertions, the capital gains lobby has produced studies by three leading econometric consulting firms. These wizards have fed the proposed tax cut into their computer models of the way the world works, and all three conclude that it would indeed produce an increase in federal tax revenues, plus myriad other benefits. There is irony in this worship of the econometric oracles, because until very recently they were a favorite target of conservatives, who accused them of burying too many "Keynesian" assumptions in their mathematical formulas. But apparently the market for prophecies responds to supply and demand just like any other. Hired by the Securities Industry Association, for example, Otto Eckstein's Data Resources, Inc. produced a conclusion that complete elimination of all tax on capital gains would add almost $200 billion to the gross national product and $38 billion to federal revenues by 1982. A recent issue of *National Review* congratulates Eckstein, a classic Kennedy Keynesian and longtime conservative *bete noir*, for having the good sense to amend his model. According to Donald Lubick, assistant Treasury secretary for tax policy, the different assumptions DRI used in an unsponsored study last year would have shown a substantial revenue *loss* from eliminating the capital gains tax.

The key to all these studies is the effect of a capital gains cut on the stock market. The DRI study for the securities industry and another study by a division of Merrill Lynch start by *assuming* that the Steiger cuts would send the stock market up by 20 percent. A study by another firm, Chase Econometric Associates, says the stock market would go up 40 percent, but this is "empirically determined from multiple regression analysis and is not simply an assumption pulled out of thin air." A Treasury Department official has charged that Chase's formula "commits several grievous statistical sins" and in particular "is guilty of multicollinearity and serial correlation, as well as improper specification." These must be fighting words to a statistician. A layman cannot know whether they are justified. But as the Treasury official suggests, if Chase Econometrics really has developed a formula that can predict the stock market, it can now comfortably retire from the econometrics-for-hire business.

Once higher stock prices are plugged into the computers, the other results follow quite straightforwardly. Higher stock prices and lower capital gains taxes encourage people to sell their stocks, which brings in tax revenues. Higher stock prices also produce lower interest rates, which stimulate investment, which increases productivity, which also brings in more tax revenues. The Chase study concludes that the Steiger cut would pay for itself by "unlocking" profitable investments that people have avoided cashing in because of the tax bite, and by generating new taxable gains on the stock market. The additional tax revenue brought in by a newly invigorated economy would be pure gravy.

But would such a narrowly based cut in the tax on potential profits from stock investments really have such a large positive effect on the stock market? Well, the general level of stock prices does represent a sort of psychological consensus about the future of the economy. So it's possible that all the propaganda in favor of a capital gains tax cut will create a self-fulfilling "prosperity illusion" (similar in operation to the Keynesian "money illusion" of which conservative economists are so skeptical): if enough people believe the tax cut will bring prosperity, the market will go up, which will help bring prosperity.

If investors (unlike members of Congress) see through the propaganda, however, the trick will not work, because there's no genuine reason why the Steiger amendment should suddenly make investing in stocks so spectacularly more attractive. It will have no effect at all on the vast majority of people with money to invest. Charles Schultze, chairman of the Council of Economic Advisers, told Congress last month that the Steiger proposal would bring America's stockholders a total of $500 million a year in tax savings, compared to their total stock investment of one trillion dollars. "How an increase in the after-tax income equal to one-half of one percent of asset values is supposed to increase those values by 20 to 40 percent escapes me," Schultze said. Taxation of capital gains represents only 10 percent of the federal tax burden on returns to capital. The corporate income tax and the regular income tax on dividends, interest, property income, etc., account for the other 90 percent. Furthermore, if the purpose of a capital gains tax cut is to encourage investment in productive assets, most of it goes completely to waste, since (according to Schultze) "the bulk of capital gains stems from sales of private homes, timber, land, jewelry, art, and similar items" unrelated to productive activity.

Adherents of the Steiger amendment supplement their computerized subtleties with a straightforward deception, comparing the alleged 49 percent maximum tax on capital gains in this country with the alleged absence of any capital gains tax in less decadent countries such as Germany and Japan. A chart making this point, put out by the W. R. Grace & Company, has popped up in newspaper ads, letters to the editor, the *Congressional Record* and other reservoirs of half-truth. It is phony. A 49 percent capital gains tax is theoretically possible for a US taxpayer, but the IRS never has found anyone who actually had to pay this much tax. The typical person pays less than a third of it. Japan taxes capital gains in full like other income, after an annual exclusion of about $1600 per taxpayer: a much tougher tax than ours. A special rule provides for a tax of at least 40 percent on profits from the sale of land and buildings. Germany has a special capital gains tax for businesses, whether incorporated or not, and has a wealth tax for individuals that applies to increases in net worth even before the asset is sold for profit. Now take Italy. *There* is a country that does not tax capital gains at all, and Portugal taxes most at only 10 percent. But somehow these countries don't seem to make it onto the charts asserting a connection between capital gains taxation and economic prosperity.

The Steiger amendment, or whatever compromise version of it gets passed, will have one particularly insidious effect that is precisely the opposite of the claims made for it, but which must be important to its supporters: it will make tax shelters much more useful. An often-heard Laffer-type argument is that lowering "high" marginal tax rates can bring in added revenue by making tax shelters more trouble than they're worth. In effect the government can offer wealthy taxpayers a chance to eliminate the middlemen—the lawyers and accountants who set up these complicated financial arrangements—and split the difference. As a bonus economic efficiency is improved by diverting money from investments that make sense only for tax purposes, and encouraging investments that meet real economic needs.

But an important function of the typical tax shelter is to convert ordinary income into capital gain. The 1969 tax reforms, which ended the 25 percent ceiling on capital gains, reduced this particular advantage of tax shelters. They put out of business some of the shelters with the least real economic value. The Steiger amendment will make these wasteful projects profitable again, thereby reducing the efficiency of the economy and losing tax revenues.

There is little reason to think that tinkering with the upper reaches of the capital gains tax will encourage productive investment or bestir sleeping entrepreneurs or increase tax revenues or do anything more than to further enrich the very few who will benefit directly from it. Channeling money and creativity into productive uses should be an important part of any tax reform. It's true that our present tax code does the opposite. A radical tax reform program should include measures such as "integrating" the corporate income tax, allowing tax-payers to "roll over" their investments without paying taxes, indexing for inflation and other measures that would increase the after-tax return to capital. These changes would move us in the direction of a "consumption tax" system that wouldn't tax income until it was withdrawn from productive use. But efficiency and fairness also would require changes that Charls Walker's clients might not find so pleasant—an end to special treatment for capital gains, closing of opportunities for tax shelters, taxing of consumption disguised as business expense (the three-martini lunch) and an inheritance tax with a real bite to prevent great accumulations of wealth.

None of this will ever happen. The tax code mirrors the defects in our political system: it enshrines the interests of organized groups, at the expense of individuals and the interest of society as a whole. Real sweeping reform is impossible. The Steiger amendment is just one more special favor that makes the tax code a bit less fair and distorts economic incentives just a bit more. No special interest is better organized than the business community. It can purchase the pages of newspapers, the minds of intellectuals and the votes of legislators. This is what the Laffer curve really teaches us about the way the world works.

2/
THE KEMP-ROTH BILL

In the name of restoring incentive to the American economy, Congressman Jack Kemp of New York and Senator William Roth of Delaware introduced the "Tax Rate Reduction Act of 1977." Supporting arguments center around the increasing tax burden and its discouraging effect on work, growth, investment, saving, and productivity. Proponents point to the added impact of suggested increases for social security, energy, and welfare, coupled with the automatic increase in taxes experienced by those pushed into higher tax brackets by inflation. It is estimated that if inflation continues as it has been, the real tax burden on each American will increase by more than 30 percent over the next four years.

The Kemp-Roth bill seeks to restore incentive in the following manner:

1. Reduce all individual income tax rates by about 33 percent
2. Reduce the corporate tax rate by 3 percentage points
3. Increase the corporate surtax exemption to $100,000

Each of these actions is to be carried out over a three-year period.

Those who oppose such a tax cut measure claim it will increase the budget deficit unless accompanied by a cut in government spending. Kemp-Roth supporters argue that the incentives that will flow from a cut in taxes will actually expand the tax base, thereby increasing tax revenues to the government. The following articles present a variety of positions on the economic impact of the Kemp-Roth bill.

The Kemp-Roth-Laffer Free Lunch

WALTER HELLER

Walter Heller, Regents' professor of economics at the University of Minnesota and former chairman of the Council of Economic Advisers under Presidents Kennedy and Johnson, questions the ability of a tax cut, such as that embodied in the Kemp-Roth bill, to generate an increase in government revenue adequate to cover the budget deficit.

Sound the trumpets and hear the heralds: There is, after all, such a thing as a free lunch! And it's not soft-headed liberals but hard-headed conservatives that bear the glad tidings.

More explicitly, it is Congressman Kemp and Senator Roth with their $114 billion tax cut bill—embraced as official GOP policy—who offer us this bonanza. On their silver platter, one finds a 33%, or $98 billion, serving of individual income tax cuts and a garnish of $15.5 billion in corporate cuts, both to be phased in over the next three years.

And it won't cost us a thin dime. According to the Kemp-Roth June 1978 "Tax Cut News," their cuts "will increase the incentive to work, save and invest, resulting in higher economic growth, lower prices, more jobs and higher government revenues." And all this happens without budget cuts, the true believers tell us. Lunch is not only free, we get a bonus for eating it. P. T. Barnum, move over.

But ridicule is not reason. One must appraise the historical, quantitative and analytical foundations on which the Kemp-Roth structure is built.

Let's start with their assertion that "the Kennedy tax cut provides the best historical proof" that their tax cut will work. In the light of Congressman Kemp's flattering references to my paternal role in the 1964 tax cut, it may be a bit graceless to say quite flatly that he has been misled both as to the cause of the Kennedy tax cut's success and as to the Treasury's supposed goof in forecasting its revenue effects.

THE RECORD IS CRYSTAL CLEAR

First, as to "verdict of history" that the Kennedy tax cut ($12 billion-plus, roughly equivalent to $36 billion today) achieved its success, to quote Mr. Kemp, "by increasing aggregate *supply* by increasing the reward to work and investment": on the contrary, the record is crystal clear that it was its stimulus to *demand*, the multiplied impact of its release of over $10 billion of consumer purchasing power and $2 billion of corporate funds, that powered the 1964–65 expansion and restored a good part of the initial revenue loss.

Walter Heller, "The Kemp-Roth-Laffer Free Lunch," *The Wall Street Journal*, July 12, 1978, p. 20. Reprinted by permission of the author and *The Wall Street Journal*, ©Dow Jones Company, Inc., 1978. All Rights Reserved.

By activating idle human and physical resources—reducing unemployment from 5.6% in January 1964 to 4.5% in July 1965 (when Vietnam escalation
began) and boosting utilization rates in manufacturing—it drew on "aggregate
supply" capacity that already existed. Inflation, which had been running at
1.4% before the tax cut, crept up to only 1.6% by the summer of 1965. The
purchasing power punch of the tax cut was thus converted into higher sales
volume, higher output, more jobs and more income, not into higher prices.

To give any credence to the Kemp-Roth thesis that the 1964 tax cut accomplished all this by unleasing incentives and triggering a great leap forward
on the supply side, one would have to find a sudden bulge in productivity and
GNP potential in the economic statistics for the mid 1960s.

No such bulge occurred. True, our 1962–1964 tax cuts were well-designed to
boost investment and work incentives (via new investment credits, more liberal
depreciation, a cut in top rates from 91% to 70% and so on). But these benign
effects on the supply side work slowly, gradually tilting the productivity growth
curve upward.

Estimates by Norman B. Ture that a Kemp-Roth tax cut would in a little
more than a year generate huge investment increases, four million new jobs,
$157 billion of added GNP and revenues exceeding pre-tax-cut levels stretch
both credulity and facts. As Rudolph Penner of the American Enterprise Institute puts it, "There can't be two or three or four times more bang in a Kemp-
Roth tax cut than we've had with any other."

Second, what about the great Treasury goof? Just one statement from the
Roth-Kemp release will illustrate how far the facts have been stretched: "Although Kennedy's Treasury department estimated a six-year revenue loss of $89
billion, his tax cuts expanded the economy so much that revenues actually
increased by $54 billion." To attribute to the 1962–64 tax cuts all the expansion
and revenue increases experienced in 1963–68 boggles the mind. Among other
things, it totally ignores (1) the huge (over-) stimulus of Vietnam expenditures
and (2) four payroll tax rates and base increases in those years as well as $6
billion of revenues from the 1966 Tax Act.

Even more inexplicably, those who put the Kemp-Roth numbers together
seized on a table the Treasury submitted to the House Banking Committee in
1968 to show what revenues would have been if (a) the economy had expanded
as rapidly as it did but (b) no 1964 tax cut had been enacted. In contrast, the
careful year-by-year comparison of Treasury revenue estimates and results they
should have made shows a six-year net discrepancy of only $22 billion (partly by
grace of compensating errors), rather than the $143 billion they assert. Those
who did the staff work for Congressman Kemp and Sen. Roth have done them
—and the cause of rational tax debate—a serious disservice.

Now, what about the other tax cuts cited by Kemp-Roth supporters as
precedents for the supply explosion that their huge tax cut is supposed to set off?

—The Andrew Mellon tax cuts of the 1920s are brought forward as evidence. "As a result [of the Mellon cuts], the period 1921–29 was one of phenomenal economic expansion. . . ." At a time when only a few million Americans
paid income taxes and federal spending was less than 5% of GNP (it was 3% in
1929), we are asked to believe that federal income tax cuts alone powered the
growth of GNP from $70 billion in 1921 to $103 billion in 1929.

—Or take another favorite precedent, the 1948 tax cuts in West Germany to which the great German expansion is attributed. As Chief of Internal Finance in our Military Government in Germany in 1947–48, "I was there." The multiple sources of expansion were (1) a tough and successful currency reform, (2) removal of rationing and wage and price controls, (3) the Marshall Plan, (4) bountiful harvests, (5) a bountiful labor supply swollen by two million refugees from Eastern Europe and (6) tax reduction and reform. Yet the whole German "economic miracle" is attributed to tax cuts.

In short, the Kemp-Roth enthusiasts rely excessively on *post hoc, ergo propter hoc* reasoning and on a one-dimensional view of the world. Have they forgotten that there is more to life than economic life, and that there is more to economics than taxes?

Now, for a look at the "Laffer Curve," a diagram designed to show how tax changes can suppress or unleash incentives to work and invest and hence affect tax revenues. The tax cuts that are cited as "evidence" have just been explored. But let me go beyond this to look at the assertion that we are so far out on the Laffer Curve that tax cuts would release enormous tax-suppressed energies. Here I would simply echo the conclusion of Mr. William Fellner of AEI: "The U.S. is not yet at high enough tax rates to produce anything like the revenue explosion that Laffer is predicting." And I would agree with him that "where the U.S. economy is along such a curve is completely undocumented, unexplored and unknown."

Have tax pressures increased sharply since the mid-60s and perhaps brought us closer to the breaking point? Comparative figures assembled regularly by the OECD show total U.S. taxes at 27.3% of GNP in 1966 and 29.6% in 1976, hardly enough of an increase for tax cuts to trigger much bigger responses today than in the mid-60s. Besides, with top income tax rates at 50% and 70% instead of 91%, there is less tax disincentive to remove.

But let's move beyond the field of taxation and take another cut at it. Broadening our horizon to include the whole range of quantitative surveys and studies of responses to changes in after-tax rewards per unit of work, savings and investment, can we find any support for the Laffer-Kemp-Roth thesis?

First, as to savings, there is little aid and comfort in "Denison's Law." Edward F. Denison of Brookings has found that U.S. gross private domestic saving has for a century held very close to 16% of GNP (adjusted to a high employment level) year in and year out in the face of high taxes, low taxes or virtually no taxes. Contrary findings about the elasticity of the savings rate still fall short of the taxpayer response predicted by proponents of Kemp-Roth.

But what about labor supply elasticity? Don't the myriad studies of the responses of workers to increases or decreases in take-home pay lend some support to the Laffer thesis that big tax cuts would stimulate a big switch from leisure to work and thus sharply increase labor supply? No.

TWO CONFLICTING RESPONSES

The human animal has two quite conflicting responses to increases in take-home pay, from whatever source. Yes, the studies show some people working harder and longer as tax cuts or other income boosts make leisure and sloth more "expensive." But others respond to an income boost by taking out some of their gains in more leisure, that is, by working less hard to gain a given target income. In economic terms, the studies tell us that the income elasticity of labor supply is not very great either way, and it is not clear whether it is, on net balance, negative or positive. So the Kemp-Roth advocates would once again look in vain for support of their belief that big tax cuts would cause a vast upsurge in labor supply.

To summarize, then, nothing in the history of tax cuts, econometric studies of taxpayer responses, or field surveys of incentives suggests that the effects of a big tax cut on the supply of output even begin to match its effects on the demand for output. A $114 billion tax cut in three years would simply overwhelm our existing productive capacity with a tidal wave of increased demand and sweep away all hopes of curbing deficits and containing inflation. Indeed, it would soon generate soaring deficits and roaring inflation.

One wonders whether these considerations are not beginning to generate some self-doubts, as they should, in the Kemp-Roth camp. Disarmingly, Laffer, as their "economic guru," recently told Newsweek: "There's more than a reasonable probability that I'm wrong. But . . . why not try something new?" Why not? One reason might be that in getting the Republican party on the Kemp-Roth hook, he may be leading it over the cliff.

Populist Remedy for Populist Abuses

IRVING KRISTOL

Many opponents of the Kemp-Roth bill are concerned over its purported inflationary ramifications and urge that the tax cut be accompanied by a cut in government spending. Irving Kirstol, Henry Luce professor of urban values at New York University and senior fellow of the American Economic Institute, addresses each of these criticisms, noting that (1) the tax cut will generate considerable economic growth and, consequently, increased government revenues and (2) if the increased revenues prove to be insufficient, our political leaders will then find it possible to cut government spending.

The spirited quarrels among economists, in The Wall Street Journal and elsewhere, about the Kemp-Roth bill are interesting—but also more than a little confusing.

That liberal economists should oppose the bill—which would slash individual income tax rates by 30% over the next three years, and slightly reduce corporate rates as well—is understandable. Most of them believe, basically, that government can spend the people's money more wisely than the people themselves. They are also committed to the egalitarian principle that affluent citizens should always pay more, never less, taxes.

That some businessmen and some business publications (e.g., Business Week and Forbes) should be distrustful of it is only a little less understandable. For a good portion of the business community still believes that national economic policy should be governed by a simple and static principle: first balance the budget by cutting government's expenditures—and then cut taxes. This is prudent bookkeeping but betrays a naive ignorance of the dynamics of political economy.

What is extraordinary, however, is that so many conservative economists have such ambivalent attitudes toward the bill. Only a few are opposed to it outright. Most of them take the odd position that the thinking behind the bill is all wrong—"the Kemp-Roth Free Lunch," Milton Friedman calls it scornfully—but they (including Dr. Friedman) support it anyway. Why so critical? And why such support, nevertheless?

THE TWO MAIN ARGUMENTS

There are two main arguments offered in favor of the Kemp-Roth bill. The first is to the effect that, without such a tax cut, and assuming an average inflation rate of 7% annually, marginal rax rates 10 years from now will be absolutely

Irving Kristol, "Populist Remedy for Populist Abuses," *The Wall Street Journal,* August 10, 1978, p. 20. Reprinted by permission of the author and *The Wall Street Journal,* © Dow Jones & Company, Inc., 1978. All Rights Reserved.

horrendous. Specifically, a four-person household with an annual income of $15,000 (in inflated dollars) in 1987 will then find itself paying a 50% tax at the margin. This would be ruinous to all economic incentives, and would probably provoke a major political convulsion as well. The Kemp-Roth tax cut would permit the taxpayer to avoid the "double whammy" created by inflation combined with the progressive income tax.

The second argument is in response to those who worry about the inflationary impact of such a tax cut at this time, and who insist that it be accompanied by substantial cuts in government spending. This argument is to the effect that, while every effort should certainly be made to hold down government spending—both Kemp and Roth, after all, are conservative Republicans—the tax cuts themselves will be so conducive to economic growth that government's revenues will eventually increase to such an extent as to make the budgetary deficit a negligible concern. And it is this issue—centering around the "Laffer curve" and its seemingly perverse promise of increased revenues through tax cuts—that creates a storm of controversy among conservative economists.

In fact, the argument from inflation, though it has a superficial plausibility, is—as Dr. Friedman would agree—beside the point. Paul Craig Roberts has shown persuasively in these pages that a cut in tax rates need not be inflationary. Inflation is a monetary phenomenon, and if the government does not finance its deficits via the printing press, there will be no inflation (though there can, of course, be other undesirable economic consequences). A tax cut can be funded by new debt, by borrowing from the public, rather than with newly-printed money.

Ah, Milton Friedman then intervenes, in that case you are not talking about a "real" tax cut at all! "The total tax burden on the American people," he writes, "is what the government spends, not those receipts called 'taxes.' And any deficit is borne by the public in the form of hidden taxes . . . ," for an increased deficit surely will have to be paid for with future tax revenues.

He is, as usual, absolutely right—from the point of view of academic economics. But academic economics is not quite the same thing as real-world economics. In the academic universe, little attention is paid to entrepreneurial innovation—an activity which, since it is not quantifiable in its extent or effects, is largely ignored by modern economic theory. Businessmen, who are growth-oriented, ought to understand this aspect of public economic policy better than they do. They are familiar enough with the example of a stagnant firm, already heavily in debt, restructuring itself internally to increase growth, and financing this process by increasing its debt in the hope that this will be more than compensated for by that future growth. In effect, Kemp-Roth represents such a restructuring and refinancing of the national economy, for purposes of growth.

That Dr. Friedman and other conservative economists nevertheless support Kemp-Roth, despite their continual sniping at it, is testimony to the fact that, if their economics is overly academic, their politics is not. They have learned the lesson of Proposition 13, which is that tax cuts are a prerequisite for cuts in government spending. The politics of the budgetary process is such that a cut in any particular program will provoke intense opposition from a minority, and only indifference from the majority. In such a case, it is unreasonable to expect politicians to pay the high political costs involved. They can only cut when they are seen to have no alternative. The Federalist Papers refers to our complicated constitutional structure, with its checks and balances, as offering a "republican remedy for the abuses of republican government." The tax-cut movement represented by Proposition 13 and Kemp-Roth can, I think, with justice be described as a populist remedy for the abuses of populist government.

But to return to the controversial though by no means central economic question: Will, in fact, the Kemp-Roth tax cut generate enough economic activity, enough growth, and a sufficiently enlarged tax base, so that government's revenues actually increase to such a degree as to close the initial budgetary gap which such a tax cut will create? The only honest answer is that we don't know—no one knows—for certain. But we do know two things for certain.

First, it will surely generate a substantial degree of economic growth and will therefore probably result in some increase in government's revenues. The theory behind the Laffer curve is validated by both current and historical experience, even if—to the annoyance of academic economists—it does not lend itself to the kind of quantification that fits neatly into their macroeconomic procedures. Thus, one picks up The New York Times for Aug. 1 and reads a story on the sports pages which begins as follows:

> "Saratoga Springs, N.Y.—With a 'new deal' tax structure taking effect, New York horseplayers turned out in record numbers today for the start of Saratoga's 24-day thoroughbred meeting.
>
> With the parimutuel take out reduced from 17% to 14%, a crowd of 21,228 showed up as America's oldest active race track opened its 110th meeting in 115 years. No first day here has ever been so busy."

MR. JONES'S TESTIMONY

As for our historical experience with tax cuts, when Reg Jones of G.E. testified before the Senate Finance Committee last year he pointed out that we have had 11 tax cuts since World War II and that, in 10 out of those 11 cases, government revenues increased within a year. In the eleventh case—1948—it took two years for that to occur.

Secondly, if government's revenues should fail to increase sufficiently, and the budgetary imbalance is not ameliorated, then (and only then) can we anticipate that our political leaders will find it possible to make sharp cuts in spending. In politics, the necessary is sometimes a precondition for the possible.

So it seems to me that, for reasons both economic and politic, the Kemp-Roth bill is exactly the right medicine for what ails us at this time. It also seems a shame that so much intellectual energy should be expended in quarrels over whether the right medicine is being prescribed for precisely the right reasons.

The Real Reasons for a Tax Cut

HERBERT STEIN

Herbert Stein is the A. Willis Robertson professor of economics at the University of Virginia, a senior fellow of the American Economic Institute, and former chairman of the Council of Economic Advisers under Presidents Nixon and Ford. While frequent support for the Kemp-Roth bill comes from "supply side" economists—those seeing it as a way to expand the economy and, therefore, government revenues through incentives provided to the productive sector—Stein supports it for different reasons. He considers the justification for Kemp-Roth to be based not on its suggested revenue-generating capabilities, but instead on the restrictive pressure he claims it will exert on the budget.

I have always thought it unfortunate that the Kemp-Roth bill was tangled up with the Laffer Curve. The claim that an across-the-board cut of income tax rates would increase the revenue was a powerful one, if true. It was so attractive that it diverted attention from the basic arguments for the bill. But some day the weakness of the claim would become apparent to all. And there was a danger that when that happened supporters and opponents of the bill would both conclude that the case for it had collapsed.

In previous articles in this journal I have expressed my skepticism about the revenue-raising claim, and I have spelled out the reasons for that skepticism in the July issue of the AEI Economist. I agree with almost everything that Walter Heller said on this subject in The Wall Street Journal of July 12, although, as is often the case, I am less certain of my beliefs than he seems to be of his.

Economists cannot say that they know with certainty that the Kemp-Roth tax cut would not raise the revenue. They can, or should, only say that the available evidence makes that outcome extremely improbable. It may turn out that such a tax cut would raise the revenue, just as it may turn out that there is human life on Mars. But I would not invest much in a McDonald's franchise on that planet, and I wouldn't bet the nation's economic policy on the assumption that the tax cut will increase the revenue.

A SIMPLE, STRONG CASE

I hope we can leave that question behind us and now focus on the real case for the Kemp-Roth bill, or some such large, broad-based tax cut to be phased in over the next several years. The case is simple and strong. The case is that when the wage-earner gets his paycheck and sees how much has been deducted for federal taxes he is shocked and enraged. It is not because he thinks that the revenue or the GNP would be higher if less were taken from him in taxes that he is enraged. It is because he earned the money fair and square. It is his. He has plenty of things that he wants to do with it. And he doesn't want the government to take so much of it away from him.

That is a genuine reaction, and it needs to be taken into account. Moreover, in my opinion, it is a legitimate reaction. In our society there is a presumption that a person is entitled to keep what he has earned. This is a rebuttable presumption. We accept the propriety of taking some of that income away from him by a democratic process to meet imperative social needs.

But the burden of proof is not on the taxpayer to show why he is entitled to keep what he has earned. It is his money. The burden of proof is on those who would tax it away from him, to show that it is needed to meet imperative social requirements.

The basic case for Kemp-Roth is the belief that this burden of proof is not being sustained, and that a large part of the taxes that are being collected now and that would be collected in the future would not be used to serve imperative social needs. What is an imperative social need is, of course, a highly debatable subject. It cannot be settled by a computer, or even by an economist. We have a democratic process for settling that question, and the Kemp-Roth bill is an appeal to that process.

It can be said that all the expenditures we make now, and all the expenditures we make in the future, have been, or will be, approved by this same democratic process, by our elected Congressmen and Presidents. There is no higher authority to which one can appeal, and therefore no basis for complaining about the present or prospective rate of spending.

But the democratic process has given the answer it has to the expenditure question because the question has been asked in a certain way. Proponents of Kemp-Roth now propound a different question, in the expectation that the democratic process will yield a different answer.

Up to now the question has been how much should we spend on this particular program this year, given the fact that the growth of the economy plus inflation have given us much more revenue this year than we had last year. This way of asking the question is tilted in the direction of bigger spending for three reasons.

First, each expenditure program receives the vigorous support of those who expect to benefit from it directly, whereas the much larger body of taxpayers who would have to pay for it see the resulting burden as negligible and do not offer effective resistance. Second, the year-to-year process leads to commitments to the future growth of expenditures which are either not seen or not appreciated when made but are hard to reverse later. Third, the automatic growth of revenue with the rise of the economy and inflation allows the government to avoid an explicit decision to raise taxes when it raises expenditures.

Advocates of the Kemp-Roth bill want to ask the question differently. They want first to ask how much of our income we should pay in taxes to the federal government three or four years from now, and then they want to ask how much we should be spending for various programs, given the answer to the first question. They believe that if the question is asked in this way the answer will be more representative of the priorities and wishes of the American people than if the question is asked in the conventional, program-by-program, year-by-year way.

The Kemp-Roth bill gives the American people and the Congress an opportunity to decide now that in 1983 they do not want to pay to the federal government more than 19% of the GNP in taxes, compared to almost 23% that they would be paying if tax rates are not reduced.

The 19% of GNP that they would be paying in 1983 if Kemp-Roth were enacted would be a little smaller fraction than they are now paying and a little larger fraction than they paid on the average in the years between the Korean war and the Vietnam war.

The issue that Kemp-Roth raises is not mainly whether tax burdens should be reduced; it is whether tax burdens should be allowed to rise substantially in the next five years.

The suggestion is sometimes made that instead of committing ourselves now to a large tax cut which would take effect in stages over several years we should only make a decision year-by-year in the light of our emerging expenditure needs. This approach has prima facie reasonableness. However, it ignores a major element in the problem.

Unless we make long-run plans we find ourselves each year facing expenditure commitments that seem to preclude any substantial reduction of tax rates. The government needs to be put on notice to plan expenditures so that its share of GNP declines to, say, 20% or 19%. We must create a situation in which proponents of new spending programs bear the burden of advocating higher tax rates, or a bigger deficit, and cannot simply dip into the pool of revenue generated by growth and inflation.

I would go beyond that and include in the tax bill a requirement that the President submit each year a budget which does not exceed a specified, declining fraction of GNP. The fraction might be 21% of fiscal 1980, 20.5% for fiscal 1981 and 20% for fiscal 1982.

Prof. Heller has warned that the Kemp-Roth bill would cause "soaring deficits and roaring inflation." The spectacle of Prof. Heller warning about deficits and inflation is a rare occurrence, like the eruption of Krakatoa, and one should pay attention to it. In deference to that I would change the timing of the Kemp-Roth cuts a little. Instead of three equal cuts, as proposed in the bill, I would make half of the first cut effective on Jan. 1, 1979, and the other half on Jan. 1, 1980, with the second full step on Jan. 1, 1981, and the final one on Jan. 1, 1982.

Of course, the usual argument against a proposal like the Kemp-Roth bill is that we can't afford it. We are said to have expenditure requirements which make it impossible for us to forego so much revenue. This takes us back to the point made at the beginning of this article. Does the taxpayer think that he is getting his money's worth out of present and prospective programs? If he doesn't think so, we can obviously afford to make the cuts. If he does think he is getting his money's worth, and will continue to get it as expenditures rise in the future, then taxes should not be cut, and the basic premise of Kemp-Roth is wrong. That is what Congress will have to decide when it votes.

A BASIC NEED

Sometimes there is an implication that aside from what the citizens or the public may prefer there are commitments to expenditures that make large tax reduction impossible. But that is not the case. If we continued to meet the costs of all the programs that were on the books in January 1978 we would still have a great deal of room for tax reduction. The basic need is to avoid the addition of new expenditure programs for a while.

The other evening I was watching President Carter on TV in the Rose Garden signing an appropriation bill for LEAA. (If you don't know what that is it doesn't matter. It could be anything.) He said that this program hadn't done much in the past, but now it was really going to work. And I thought of how many times I had heard that in the past.

I said to my wife, "Next week I'm going to testify before a congressional committee and they're going to ask me 'Where would you cut the budget?' as if there were no possible answer, and I will say, 'Everywhere,'" "Everywhere but defense," she corrected me—right as usual. And that's the spirit that justifies Kemp-Roth.

The Economic Case for Kemp-Roth

PAUL CRAIG ROBERTS

In response to Stein's and Heller's editorials on the Kemp-Roth bill, Paul Craig Roberts puts forth an argument in favor of Kemp-Roth, concentrating on its incentive effects—the "economics of supply." Roberts is associate editor of *The Wall Street Journal*, senior research fellow at the Hoover Institution at Stanford University, and adjunct professor of economics at George Mason University. He is former economic counsel to Senator Orrin Hatch (R., Utah).

Walter Heller is known to the public as a liberal economist who was Chairman of the Council of Economic Advisers under a Democratic President, and Herbert Stein as a conservative economist who held the same position under Republican Presidents. Both agree that the Kemp-Roth tax rate reduction bill is economic nonsense. "It would soon generate soaring deficits and roaring inflation," says Mr. Heller. "I agree," says Mr. Stein.

Before the public is misled by their agreement into concluding that there is no economic case to be made for Kemp-Roth, I would like to show that there is.

Profs. Heller and Stein both think of tax cuts in Keynesian terms of the dollar amount put into the economy to fuel spending. They believe tax cuts work by raising the disposable income of consumers, who then spend more. The increased spending soaks up excess capacity and unemployed labor, thus moving the economy to higher levels of employment and GNP. The Kemp-Roth bill is, in their view, too large a tax cut. They believe it would fuel more new spending than there is excess capacity and produce an inflationary excess demand.

As Mr. Heller put it on this page July 12, the bill would "simply overwhelm our existing productive capacity with a tidal wave of increased demand." A smaller tax cut, he thinks, would be in order. In his July 18 article, Mr. Stein agreed with this economic analysis, but supported Kemp-Roth as a desperate means of forcing a reduction in federal spending.

A CURIOUS ANALYSIS

This economic analysis, first of all, is a curious one for economists who believe that tax cuts work by increasing demand. Without Kemp-Roth, taxes will increase due to automatic tax increases caused by inflation and higher Social Security taxes: one would expect Keynesians to be worrying about the need to offset the depressing effects of "fiscal drag."

In the context of ongoing tax increases, the Kemp-Roth reductions in the personal income tax rates do not amount to much in dollar terms. Net of the tax increases, Kemp-Roth is a $2 billion cut in 1979, a $15 billion cut in 1980, an $18 billion cut in 1981, a $7.5 billion cut in 1982 and a $1 billion cut in 1983—hardly enough to overwhelm the nation's productive capacity with a tidal wave of consumer spending. Keynesians ought to believe that the net additions to demand provided by Kemp-Roth are too small to have much impact on the economy, just as Mr. Heller says that the Mellon cuts of the 1920s were too small in dollar terms to have had any relation to the prosperity that followed.

The economic case for Kemp-Roth, though, does not rest on increasingly dubious Keynesian premises about government policy "injecting" spending to add to aggregate demand. Like the Mellon tax cuts, it is based on incentive effects, on the economics of supply. As the adage goes, it is hard to teach old dogs new tricks, and Keynesians, who have spent four decades thinking in terms of spending and demand, find it hard to understand arguments about incentive and supply.

The new supply economists think of tax rate changes as incentive changes, not as income changes. To understand the difference, consider the removal of a tariff that is high enough to prevent trade in a commodity. When the tariff is lifted, no revenues are lost, no budget deficits result and no money is put into anyone's hands. Yet clearly economic activity will expand, because the disincentive is removed. Nothing in Keynesian theory captures this effect.

Yet this is in fact how tax cuts work. A tax rate reduction does not in itself produce more real goods and services. There cannot be more income unless people produce more; the only way a tax cut can boost GNP is by providing an incentive for more production. If people respond to tax cuts by working less, as Mr. Heller suggests, the GNP would fall and Keynesian fiscal policy wouldn't work either!

When tax rates are reduced, the after-tax rewards to saving, investing and working for taxable income rise. People switch into these activities out of leisure, consumption, tax shelters and working for nontaxable income. The incentive effects cause an increase in the market supply of goods and services—thus the name "supply side economics."

Consider first the choice between working for additional taxable income and enjoying additional leisure. The price to the person of additional leisure is the amount of income, after tax, that he gives up by not working. Obviously, the higher the tax rate he faces, the cheaper leisure is in terms of the income he sacrifices. In our nation with its substantial income cushions, work disincentives are not limited to the top tax brackets. Studies by Martin Feldstein of Harvard show that the lack of a significant gap between after-tax take-home pay and untaxed unemployment benefits has made leisure a free good for one million workers, thus shrinking GNP and the tax base by the value of their lost production.

Consider next the choice between working for taxable and nontaxable income. Take the case of a carpenter facing a 25% tax rate. For an additional day's earnings of $100 he gets to keep $75. Suppose that his house needs painting and a painter costs $80 a day. Since his after-tax earnings are only $75, he saves $5 by painting his own house and chooses not to earn the additional $100. Alternatively, the carpenter and painter may swap services, but either way the tax base is smaller by $180, and the government loses tax revenues.

Studies by Gary Becker of the University of Chicago have made it clear that capital and labor are employed by households to produce nontaxable income through nonmarket activities, such as a carpenter painting his own house. The amount of household-owned capital and labor supplied in the market is affected by tax rates. The higher they are, the more households allocate their resources to the production of nontaxable income.

Now consider the decision between using income for current consumption or saving and investing it for future income. The price to the person of enjoying additional current consumption is the amount of future income he forgoes. The higher the tax rate, the smaller the amount of after-tax future income he sacrifices by enjoying additional current consumption.

Take the case of a person facing the 70% tax rate on investment income. He can choose to invest $50,000 at a 10% rate of return, which would bring him $5,000 per year of additional income before taxes. Or he can choose to spend $50,000 on a Rolls-Royce. Since the after-tax value of $5,000 is only $1,500, he can enjoy a fine motor car by giving up only that amount. Britain's 98% tax rate on "unearned" (investment) income has reduce the cost of the Rolls-Royce in terms of forgone income to only $100 a year. The profusion of Rolls-Royces seen in England today is mistaken as a sign of prosperity.

Walter Heller tells us, though, that the decision to save does not depend on the relative prices of current consumption and future income; that "Denison's Law" shows that savings do not respond to higher after-tax rewards. But the most recent empirical studies of the responsiveness of savings are those of Michael Boskin of Stanford, who concludes that "private saving is indeed strongly affected by changes in the real after-tax rate of return." He specifically dismisses "Denison's Law" as a "conjecture based on evidence which is flimsy at best and dangerously misleading at worst." A current understanding of the Kemp-Roth bill's effect on savings is absolutely crucial to assessing an asserted inflationary effect.

To summarize the above points: With so many decisions affected by tax rates, it is obvious that the market supply of goods and services must respond to changes in tax rates. Our economy functions because people respond to changes in relative prices: the price of butter relative to that of margarine, beef relative to chicken, capital relative to labor and so on. A tax rate change is just another relative price change. It changes the prices of leisure and current consumption in terms of forgone current and future income. To claim that people don't respond to these price changes goes against the basic principles of economic science. Yet there is no recognition of such response in the brand of economics now used to brand Kemp-Roth as wildly inflationary.

Since Mr. Heller goes out of his way to criticize those of us who have done staff work on the Kemp-Roth bill, he should be especially interested in the results of the congressional staff debates on these points over the past year. The Congressional Budget Office, like the Treasury, once habitually offered simplistic revenue estimates that omitted the expanded tax base and revenue feedbacks. These static revenue estimates are now discredited. CBO Director Alice Rivlin has been forced to admit that her models, based on familiar Keynesian principles, are "unable to provide estimates of the long-run impact of tax cuts."

(By the way, Prof. Heller's own staff work could use some polishing. The numbers he attributed to Norman Ture do not come from Mr. Ture.)

Mr. Heller and Mr. Stein believe the Kemp-Roth bill depends on stimulating GNP sufficiently that government revenues will not fall even in the first year, thus avoiding an inflationary deficit. In arguing that feedbacks are not large enough to recover all revenues, they are demolishing a straw man. This is not what the bill's proponents mean when they say it would pay for itself. Part of the projected deficit will indeed be eliminated by revenue from the larger GNP. The remaining deficit will not be inflationary because it will be self-financing.

Deficits are linked in the public mind with inflation or crowding out because the deficits of the past decade have originated from increased government spending and tax rebates—fiscal policies designed to increase demand, not incentives. These deficits add to the demand for funds in the financial markets, thus pushing up interest rates. The Federal Reserve then adds to the money supply, monetizing the deficit in an effort to avoid rising interest rates and crowding out, and this excessive money creation causes inflation.

While Keynesian eyes can see no difference between these deficits and deficits caused by cutting taxes, in terms of incentives this difference is decisive. Lower tax rates increase after-tax rates of return, which in turn expand private savings. When Mr. Boskin's measures of the responsiveness of savings are applied to the Kemp-Roth bill, they predict an increase in gross savings of $35 billion in the first year and a steady growth thereafter. Mr. Ture has even higher estimates of the savings effect, as does Chase Econometrics.

Savings, of course, represent the supply of funds in the financial markets. So deficits caused by tax rate cuts add to the supply of funds as well as the demand for funds. This allows the deficit to be financed without pressure on interest rates and money creation. There is no need to monetize the deficit and thus no inflationary effect. In addition, the larger GNP also means higher revenues for state and local governments and corporations, which reduce their own borrowings and ease pressure in the financial markets.

THE CHASE FORECAST

Chase Econometrics has considered all of these effects in studying the effect of the Kemp-Roth bill. Chase forecasts that the federal government would recover in revenue reflows 41% of the $25 billion tax cut in the first year. This rises to 72% in the seventh year. The remaining deficit is more than covered by the increase in personal savings, retained earnings, and state and local government surplus. Thus the deficit puts no pressure on credit markets. The tax cut generates enough new savings to finance the deficit plus an increase in private investment.

It is theoretically true, of course, that government spending could increase rapidly enough to soak up all additional savings and restore pressure to monetize the deficit. But if government spending in real terms could be held to current levels for about two years, the Kemp-Roth bill would get us out of the high deficit, high inflation, low productivity, low growth doldrums, and save transfer programs like Social Security.

As for Mr. Stein, many proponents of Kemp-Roth agree with him that government spending is already too high, but this is a separate issue. Legislatively, tax bills are separate from spending bills, and there is no way to tie them together. The only purpose that could be served by the bill's sponsors calling for accompanying spending cuts would be to threaten the vested interests of the congressional spending committees and their constituents, leaving the bill hostage to a bitter and quite unnecessary political fight.

As for Mr. Heller, he does better when he takes off the Keynesian blinders and relies on his own experience with the Kennedy tax cuts. In his article on Kemp-Roth he says, "To attribute to the 1962–64 tax cuts all the expansion and revenue increases in 1963–68 boggles the mind. It totally ignores the huge (over-) stimulus of the Vietnam expenditures." In other words, the tax cut did not pay for itself. But he saw these events differently in testifying before the Joint Economic Committee in February 1977.

ANTICIPATING THE LAFFER CURVE

In his testimony Prof. Heller anticipated the Laffer Curve, saying that the Kennedy cut "was the major factor that led to our running a $3 billion surplus by the middle of 1965 before escalation in Vietnam struck us. It was a $12 billion tax cut which would be about $33 or $34 billion in today's terms, and within one year the revenues into the federal Treasury were already above what they had been before the tax cut." He concluded, "Did it pay for itself in increased revenues? I think the evidence is very strong that it did."

On this point Mr. Denison has something interesting to say. His estimate of the gap between actual and potential GNP for 1962 and 1963 is only $12 billion—the size of the Kennedy tax cut. Obviously, such a small gap left little room for an expansion based on increased demand and unused capacity. If Mr. Denison is correct, the substantial expansion that followed the tax cut had to be based on something else, a supply-side response to the higher after-tax rates of return.

Far from being wildly inflationary even with little unused capacity in 1962, the Kennedy tax cuts promoted healthy and noninflationary expansion. Once demand management is forgotten and incentive effects are understood, there is every reason to believe the Kemp-Roth tax cuts would do the same.

Taxes, Inflation, and the Rich

MICHAEL K. EVANS

Michael K. Evans, president of Chase Econometrics, Inc., assesses the Kemp-Roth bill in terms of its revenue-generating capacity via lowering the marginal tax rate on upper-income individuals. He documents his analysis through figures showing the increase in income tax paid by taxpayers with incomes of $100,000 or more following the Kennedy tax cut of 1964.

Increasing numbers of economists have recently suggested that massive tax cuts would cure the ailments of the U.S. economy by increasing productivity, raising incentives and hence expanding aggregate supply. The idea of supply-side incentives has been embodied in proposals like the Steiger amendment to cut capital gains taxes and the Kemp-Roth bill for an across-the-board tax cut.

These bills, and the new supply-side thinking, raise issues that sound startling in the context of contemporary economic thought: Is it possible to cut taxes without spurring inflation? And is it possible to cut taxes, or at least certain taxes, without even reducing total revenues received by the federal Treasury?

The historical record clearly indicates that the rate of inflation is inversely proportional to the gap between actual and maximum potential GNP. So measures that raise potential GNP would reduce inflation at the same time they increase economic growth. Measures that succeeded in expanding the gap by raising potential would clearly offer greater benefits to society than the traditional remedies of fiscal and monetary restraint, which expand the gap by reducing aggregate demand.

HOW A TAX CUT REDUCES INFLATION

In order for a tax cut to reduce inflation, it must increase maximum potential GNP faster than actual GNP. This is accomplished only by raising the investment ratio or by increasing incentives to work because a larger proportion of income will remain after taxes. Not all tax cuts accomplish this. A tax reduction of $50 per person, for example, would have no measurable effect on productivity or incentives, so it would not raise potential GNP. However, it would increase actual GNP, hence reducing the gap and raising the rate of inflation.

Thus the other extreme, a reduction in corporate income taxes or capital gains taxes would initially affect investment, thereby leading to the desired effect on productivity and total supply. While actual GNP would obviously rise because of higher capital spending, the gap would increase, thereby reducing

Michael K. Evans, "Taxes, Inflation, and the Rich," *The Wall Street Journal*, August 7, 1978, p. 10. Reprinted by permission of *The Wall Street Journal*, ©Dow Jones & Company, Inc., 1978. All Rights Reserved.

the rate of inflation. A number of studies by Chase Econometrics and others have already shown the salutary impacts of business tax cuts.

The question of personal income tax cuts, which has become particularly relevant in view of the increased interest in the Kemp-Roth bill, is a much more difficult one to answer. While it may be theoretically appealing to argue that a reduction in personal income taxes encourages an individual to work harder and thus increase both his pretax and aftertax income, little evidence has been assembled either to support or disprove this hypothesis.

One of the major problems is measuring the amount and intensity of work offered by an individual taxpayer. However, a reasonable proxy variable is the amount of income taxes paid by this individual. Thus we can examine what happened to federal personal income taxes by income classification in the years following major tax cuts. These occurred in the mid-1920s, under Treasury Secretary Andrew W. Mellon, and in 1964–65. It is interesting to examine both of these periods in some detail.

Before the U.S. entered World War I, the maximum tax rate on personal income was 15%, but this rate rose dramatically to a peak of 73% in 1918 and succeeding years. It was then cut to 55% in 1922 and 25% in 1926. It is instructive to learn what happened to taxes paid by millionaires—that group which has been singled out by President Carter and Treasury Secretary Blumenthal as unworthy of further tax relief. To adjust for the differentials caused by inflation, we consider those taxpayers with incomes over $300,000 in 1922 and in 1927, although even this adjustment is an understatement of the true effects of rising prices. In 1922, this group paid taxes of $77 million, while in 1927, the year after the second reduction in rates, its members paid a total of $230 million. Not only did the economy benefit significantly, but the millionaires themselves paid three times as much in taxes with lower rates.

It could be argued that the Mellon tax cut results, while instructive, are not relevant today since the institutional structure and income distribution of the U.S. economy are far different now than they were in the 1920s. However, we need not be restricted to a reading of "ancient history" in our determination of how a reduction in top bracket rates might affect overall revenues. Fortunately we can rely on the figures before and after the Kennedy-Johnson tax cuts of 1964.

As most readers will recall, the top rate was reduced from 91% in 1963 to 77% in 1964 and 70% in 1965 and later years. The figures for actual income tax paid for the period 1961–1966 for taxpayers with incomes of $100,000 or more are taken from "Statistics of Income" and are reproduced in the accompanying table.

	1961	1962	1963	1964	1965	1966
Maximum tax rate	91%	91%	91%	77%	70%	70%
Taxes collected from						
Income classes of*			(in millions $)			
Over 1,000,000	342	311	326	427	603	590
500,000-1,000,000	297	243	243	306	408	457
100,000-500,000	1970	1740	1890	2220	2752	3176

*Adjusted gross income.

The results are so clear-cut that it is surprising that these figures have not previously been introduced as evidence in favor of Kemp-Roth. After virtually no growth in income taxes for incomes over $100,000 for three years, actual taxes paid rose dramatically beginning in 1964 even though income was taxed at significantly lower rates. In the case of individuals earning over $1 million per year, taxes collected actually doubled in the two-year span during which the tax rates were being lowered. For income classes under $100,000, taxes either fell or rose less than the average growth in total personal income.

These results, which represent a remarkable rebuttal of those who argue that upper-income tax cuts are a "raid on the Treasury," indicate that a further reduction from 70% to 50% would not only spur economic growth and increase aggregate supply, but would actually assure the Treasury of greater tax revenues. The argument for upper-income tax cuts is almost as watertight as the argument for lower capital gains taxes.

The more extreme proponents of Kemp-Roth have sometimes seemed to suggest that this phenomenon occurs at all income levels. It does not, as can be seen by a perusal of the complete "Statistics of Income" figures, and by the fact that aggregate personal income tax collections did decline from $51.5 billion in 1963 to $48.6 billion in 1964. This should come as no great surprise: The effects on individual incentives and supply of labor are undoubtedly much greater where taxes are highest—at the upper income levels rather than for the typical wage earner.

FLEXIBILITY FOR UPPER INCOME GROUP

Furthermore, just as has been shown in recent work on capital gains taxes, upper income individuals have far greater flexibility in arranging the income for their assets in the form of tax-free or tax-sheltered income when tax rates are at punitively high levels. The risks of unreported income become relatively much smaller when tax rates are near 100%, and the lure of diverting earnings to foreign countries becomes much greater.

Thus if the Treasury wants to collect more revenues, it will lower the highest marginal tax brackets. Only if it wants less revenue and poorer economic growth so badly that it is willing to penalize all those "millionaires" will it push for higher upper-income tax rates.

Jack Kemp Wants to Cut Your Taxes—A Lot

IRWIN ROSS

Jack Kemp has gone from star quarterback to foremost tax-cutter and dominant policy-shaper of the Republican party. This profile by Irwin Ross portrays the means by which Kemp has helped to popularize incentive-oriented, or "supply side," economics along with his tax cut bill.

Jack Kemp is a most unusual Congressman. Members of Congress come from a variety of fields, but very few were professional athletes. Kemp was: in the middle 1960s he ranked among the outstanding quarterbacks in pro football. Most Congressmen read a lot, of necessity, but relatively few are heavy readers of serious books. Kemp is: he's a dedicated, not to say compulsive, student of economics. Few members of Congress emerge as national figures without quite a lot of seniority behind them. Kemp did: regarded as merely a curiosity after his football stardom catapulted him into Congress in 1970, he has become a political star, a spokesman for his party and a molder of its policies.

A man of missionary zeal, Kemp is involved in no less daunting an effort than trying to reshape the thrust and strategy of the Republican party. He wants to drop the old rhetoric about cutting spending and balancing the budget and instead rally the voters with a new battle cry of jobs and economic expansion through big tax cuts. He has already had a remarkable impact. Last fall, the Kemp-Roth tax-reduction bill (co-authored by Republican Senator William Roth of Delaware) was unanimously endorsed by the Republican National Committee. It has picked up more than 160 cosponsors in the Congress.

Kemp has become one of the G.O.P.'s most sought-after speakers; since last September he has carried his campaign to nineteen states, averaging better than a speech a week. He is featured in the Republican National Committee's twenty-eight-minute TV film on tax cuts, and has been invited to address fourteen Republican state conventions (not all of which can be fitted into his schedule).

ECHOES OF J.F.K.

Kemp's program has a bold and dramatic sweep to it. His bill calls for a deep across-the-board cut in personal income-tax rates—an average of 30 percent, to be phased in over a three-year period. By comparison, the tax-rate cut that President Carter recently proposed is positively niggling. The Kemp-Roth bill also calls for a mild reduction in the top corporate rate, from 48 to 45 percent over three years, as well as an increase in the threshold—from $50,000 to $100,000—at which the top corporate rate takes effect.

Kemp makes much of the point that his tax program is modeled after the Kennedy cuts of 1964-65, which reduced income-tax rates nearly 20 percent and

Irwin Ross, "Jack Kemp Wants to Cut Your Taxes—A Lot." Reprinted from the April 10, 1978 issue of FORTUNE Magazine, pp. 37–40, by special permission; ©1978 Time Inc.

cut the corporate rate from 52 to 48 percent. In Kemp's view, the Kennedy cuts were a tremendous success in reviving incentives and stimulating the economy. He frequently uses the slogan, "Let's get the economy moving again," echoing the theme of John F. Kennedy's 1960 presidential campaign. The Republican film on taxes actually includes a clip of J.F.K. presenting his tax program to a joint session of Congress in January, 1963. The frequency with which Kemp invokes Kennedy suggests that the late President may be passing into the pantheon of nonpartisan national heroes. At the same time, of course, Kemp is making an effort to deflect Democratic flak directed against his tax plan.

BEYOND BLOCK-THAT-DEFICIT

There is a touch of irony in Kemp's advocacy of grand-scale tax reduction. He has generally been identified with the conservative wing of his party. He worked briefly for Ronald Reagan during his time as governor of California, was an ardent hawk on Vietnam, and has tended to take a right-wing position on most issues—for example, against ratification of the Panama Canal treaties and against decriminalization of marijuana. Early in his congressional career he introduced a constitutional amendment to prohibit busing.

His tax program, however, is anything but conservative, if that label is taken to signify old-fashioned, block-that-deficit fiscal conservatism. Indeed, in speaking of his economic views, Kemp occasionally refers to himself as a radical, by which he means that he gets at the roots of things. Conservatives, of course, would like to lower taxes, but they worry about the budgetary consequences and therefore want tax cuts to be accompanied by spending cuts. Kemp, while making an occasional reference to "prudent spending," does not propose any reduction in outlays.

"I don't worship at the shrine of the balanced budget," he says. "Republicans have been trying to balance the budget ever since Herbert Hoover. I would much rather have a growing economy and a budget that's unbalanced than a contracting economy with a balanced budget." He is well aware that in a growing economy, stimulated by tax cuts, the relative proportions of private and public spending would shift in the direction of the former, but he does not stress the point.

"SO THEY ELECTED ME"

On the platform the boyish-looking, powerfully built Kemp is a rousing performer. He will start out conversationally, but as he warms to his theme he is soon bouncing around behind the podium, rearing back one moment, jutting forward another, and continually using his hands—to form globes, trace soaring arcs, or emphasize points with an outstretched finger, a slicing motion, or a clenched fist pounding the air.

Before he gets to the main business, he indulges in some genial self-deprecation. He recalls, for example, that when he was first running for Congress, he told a TV interviewer that he'd probably return to football if he lost the election. That night, as Kemp tells it, a newscaster solemnly reported that "congressional candidate Jack Kemp warned the people of Buffalo that if he is not elected, he will play football." Kemp adds: "So they elected me." The crowd roars.

The economic message, when it comes, is delivered in short, staccato bursts. Kemp has a number of favorite bits, which also pepper his conversation. Among them: "Generally speaking, if you tax something, you get less of it. If you subsidize something, you get more of it. In America, we tax work, growth, investment, employment, savings, and productivity, while subsidizing non-work, consumption, welfare, and debt."

To explain the impact of high marginal tax rates on incentives and output: "Let's say your income is taxed 10 percent on Monday, 20 percent on Tuesday, 30 percent on Wednesday, 40 percent on Thursday, 50 percent on Friday, and so on. For most people, sometime around Friday, you'd decide not to work anymore." Kemp feels that he can be allowed such simplistic formulations, for, as he frequently points out, "I'm not an economist. I have no formal training in economics. But I am an expert in incentives."

IN FAVOR OF WORK

While Kemp is well aware of the political attractiveness of cutting taxes, he also offers a respectable, though disputed, economic rationale for his program. Simply stated, the argument is that substantial cuts in tax rates would lead to a bigger G.N.P. by increasing people's preference for work, saving, and entrepreneurial risk-taking—as against leisure, spending, and less productive forms of investment, such as real-estate speculation. A faster-growing economy would ultimately increase government revenues, even at lower tax rates, because there would be a larger volume of private and corporate income to tax. This line of argument—from the "supply side" rather than the "demand side," as economists put it—descends from classical theory, and specifically the views of the nineteenth-century French economists Jean Baptiste Say and Leon Walras. A modern version has been put forward in recent years by Robert A. Mundell of Columbia and Arthur B. Laffer of the University of Southern California.

In setting forth his ideas, Kemp makes use of the "Laffer curve," which he is continually drawing on paper napkins and the backs of envelopes. The curve . . . illustrates the relationship between tax rates and government revenue. Very high rates of taxation limit revenue by restraining output. Lowering tax rates from such counterproductive levels can increase government revenue by stimulating greater output. That is why Kemp has no fear that his tax proposals would result in a bigger federal deficit.

In Kemp's view, the Kennedy cuts proved the efficacy of this approach. Now incentives have to be restimulated once again—because over the intervening years inflation has greatly increased the tax bite, in real terms, by pushing people into higher marginal brackets.

To support his case, Kemp points to what happened after the Kennedy tax cuts went into effect. Last year he asked the Library of Congress to compare the revenue the Treasury projected back in 1963, when Kennedy proposed his program, with what actually happened. The Treasury forecast a revenue loss of $89 billion for the years 1963–68. As things turned out, tax revenues increased by $54 billion, because of the great acceleration in economic activity. What we did before, Kemp is fond of saying, we can do again.

His economic advisers are split on what Kemp's tax cuts would do to the budget deficit. Laffer believes the Kennedy experience would be repeated. Norman Ture, a Washington consultant on whom Kemp also relies, has put the Kemp-Roth tax cuts through his econometric model, which has a heavy emphasis on supply-side effects, and comes up with a revenue gain of $1 billion in 1978 (assuming the program was already in effect) but a revenue loss of $40 billion in 1980 and $43 billion in 1982.

Ture's explanation is that in the first year there would be a sizable jump in G.N.P., as underutilized plant capacity is put to fuller use, but that in successive years the growth of G.N.P. would be slower. Nonetheless, Ture projects such a vast increase in savings that the additional deficit could be financed without any "crowding out" of private investment—a point that Kemp has seized on.

Keynesians, of course, also consider the Kennedy cuts to have been a huge success, but in their view the crucial element was expansion of demand. They argue that the effect of tax cuts on incentives has not been proved, at least in the tax environment in the U.S. For his part, Kemp says that "Kennedy's economists did the right thing for the wrong reasons." He will only grudgingly concede any stimulative effect from enlarged demand.

The political irony is that the Republican party is now on record for big tax cuts, whereas the Democratic Administration is proposing modest nicks in personal income-tax rates, and other changes that, as Kemp sees it, only increase the progressivity of the tax schedule and lead to "income redistribution rather than income growth." Many Democrats think Kemp is being demagogic and absurdly heedless of a ballooning deficit; Kemp thinks the Democrats are prisoners of false dogma.

"YOU'RE NOT SUPPOSED TO LAUGH"

The Kemp-Roth bill, of course, will not pass; such proposals by the minority party never do. But it may well raise the ante in the tax debate, for there is already a disposition among Democrats to go beyond the Carter Administration's program.

Meantime, Jack Kemp has begun to alter the face that the Republican party presents to the world. In the process, he has become a national leader of the party. Recently he has been urged to run for governor of New York this year, but that would be very chancy. Besides, the political argument he is interested in is centered in Washington. The next move he freely talks about is to the Senate in 1980, if Jacob Javits, now seventy-three, retires.

Some of Kemp's admirers see him on the national ticket two years hence, possibly even as a presidential candidate. This suggestion was reported to him somewhat jocularly a few weeks ago. "You're not supposed to laugh at that," said Kemp, not laughing. Even if his staffers share that view, however, they have been avoiding use of his middle initial (F for French, his grandmother's maiden name) or of his three initials, which have a certain familiarity: J.F.K.

3/
THE NATIONAL ENERGY PLAN

President Carter's National Energy Plan was unquestionably the focal point of the nation's attention when it was announced in April 1977. Its many facets would potentially affect every group in America—from homeowners to corporations, from consumers to producers, from East Coast residents to West Coast residents.

Carter sought to solve America's energy problems through a series of taxes and rebates aimed at inducing the American public to conserve fuel. The following is a brief summary of some of the major proposals.

To encourage conservation as it relates to transportation, the plan calls for a graduated excise tax on new automobiles and light-duty trucks, beginning with 1978 models, that fail to meet fuel-economy standards. Those vehicles that surpass the standards would receive graduated rebates. A standby gasoline tax is to take effect if targets for gasoline consumption are not met. Removal of the 10 percent excise tax on intercity buses due to their fuel efficiency, and elimination of the federal excise tax privilege for general aviation and motorboat fuel, are also included in the plan.

To curtail energy use in buildings, the program calls for a homeowner's tax credit for taking approved conservation measures in the home and government-subsidized loans to help finance those improvements. Beginning in 1980, mandatory efficiency standards will be required of new residential and commercial buildings, and existing federal buildings must reduce their energy use by 1985 by 20 percent of 1975 energy consumption and by 45 percent for new federal buildings. The government will spend $100 million over a three-year period in an effort to equip as many federal buildings as possible with solar hot water and space heating.

Increasing energy efficiency in home appliances will be attempted by requiring that certain appliances meet mandatory efficiency standards. The current program of developing test procedures and establishing labeling requirements will continue.

Existing plants that invest in approved energy-saving industrial equipment would receive a five-year, 10 percent investment tax credit.

Suggestions for conservation-encouraging changes in utility pricing policies include the phasing out and elimination of promotional and declining block rates, the option of off-peak rates for customers, and the prohibition of master metering in new structures.

In an effort to provide prices that encourage conservation and conversion to coal while preventing industry from "receiving windfall profits," the plan calls for the continuing use of price ceilings plus a tax on domestically produced oil that will increase over a three-year period, bringing the ceiling price plus tax equal to the world price. In order to bring natural gas up to the price of oil, the price ceiling on new interstate natural gas would be raised, and intrastate natural gas would then become subject to a price ceiling. The cost of the more expensive new gas will be allocated to industrial users rather than to residential and commercial users.

These proposals, along with the rest of the plan, have created tremendous controversy among business people, economists, politicians, and the press. A sample of those opinions follows.

Statement Prepared for the Ad Hoc Energy Committee

W. MICHAEL BLUMENTHAL

W. Michael Blumenthal, secretary of the Treasury, analyzes President Carter's National Energy Plan in terms of its effect on the domestic economy and on the balance of payments in his testimony before the Ad Hoc Energy Committee.

The broad economic effects of the National Energy Plan proposed by President Carter have been described by Mr. Schultze and there is no need for me to repeat his assessment, with which I concur. I will address myself to other aspects of the plan.

Some may be surprised that so comprehensive a program—involving as it does billions of dollars of additional tax collections and billions of dollars of disbursements—is projected to have such relatively small net impact on the nation's output and prices. The answer is that the plan is designed that way.

The plan has as its objective conservation and substitution—conservation of increasingly scarce resources through a reduction in the rate of growth in energy consumption, and substitution by conversion from energy sources which are limited and variable in supply to those which are domestically more abundant. The principal mechanism for achieving these objectives is the use of the tax system, through a combination of tax penalties and tax incentives. The plan has been designed so that, for the economy as a whole, the revenues collected under the proposed tax penalties will be recycled to finance related elements of the energy conservation program.

Let me illustrate. To conserve gasoline, the National Energy Plan proposes a graduated excise tax on automobiles with fuel efficiency below average. But the taxes collected would be disbursed through graduated rebates on new cars with mileage better than the standard. Another illustration: producer prices of domestic oil will be lifted in stages to the world prices of oil. But the difference between the producer price—adjusted for inflation—and the world price would be returned to consumers in the form of per capita energy credits. Another illustration: a penalty tax would be imposed on the use of oil and natural gas for industrial consumers and utilities, deferred until 1979 for industrial firms and to 1983 for utilities. But the cost of conversion to coal or other energy sources would be offset in part by a rebate of the penalty tax paid currently or, in some cases, by additional investment tax credits. The remaining proceeds of this tax would go into general revenues, and could be used to finance the buildup of a strategic petroleum reserve, and another large share could finance tax incentives for energy conservation in residential construction and similar activities.

W. Michael Blumenthal, "Statement Prepared for the Ad Hoc Energy Committee," May 1977.

Despite the rigorous effort to fashion a program with minimal impact on the general price level and on the overall economic growth rate of the country, it is clear that an effort so large and so vital must have certain costs. There will undoubtedly be transition problems as our society adjusts to a lower rate of growth in energy consumption, and to growing dependence on sources of energy other than oil and natural gas.

The automobile industry will have to accelerate its efforts to develop more fuel efficient vehicles, and this may require additional investment in research and new production facilities. Industries that wish to avoid the burden of penalty taxes on the use of natural gas and petroleum fuels by conversion to coal will have to incur investment costs which may not wholly be compensated by the rebate of the penalty tax or by an additional investment tax credit. If gasoline consumption grows too rapidly, a gasoline tax would be triggered; this tax would be recycled largely through the income tax structure, in order to maintain the real income of the consumer sector, but it is possible that the resultant rise in gasoline prices could adversely affect auto sales without a compensating rise in expenditures for other consumer goods and services. And there will undoubtedly be other transition problems and costs difficult to anticipate or measure at this point in time.

Nor is it possible to project precisely the magnitude of tax revenues and government outlays stemming from the various elements in the plan. In part, the size of the revenue and disbursement flows depends on the extent to which consumers and businesses respond to the tax penalties and tax incentives provided. Taking likely response rates into account, it is estimated that, over the period out to 1985, additional Budget outlays associated with the National Energy Plan would aggregate some $50 billion, while revenues raised by new energy-related taxes (net of credits and certain rebates) would sum to about $51 billion.

Thus, the *net* dollar impact on Federal finances, at a first approximation, would be less than $1 billion. Even the flows on each side of the Budget of some $50 billion, cumulated over the period to 1985, are small relative to an economy as large as ours.

In the near term there would be a measurable budgetary impact. In FY [fiscal year] 1978, the increase in outlays under the program would exceed the increase in revenues, thereby adding about $1½ billion to the Budget deficit. However, this is a relatively small addition, particularly so in light of the national benefits that will accrue from a prompt start on our conservation objectives. Nor will it detract from achieving our goal of a balanced budget by FY 1981.

The principal source of additonal revenues under the National Energy Plan is estimated to be the crude oil equalization tax, which over the period ending in 1985 is projected to yield about $86½ billion. All of this will be returned to the economy: about $59 billion to heating oil purchasers and income tax payers, about $13½ billion as cash payments to nonpayers, and about $14 billion in reduced business income tax payments.

The next largest source of Federal revenues stemming from the National Energy Plan will be the oil and natural gas conservation tax. This tax is intended to encourage conversion by industrial enterprises and utilities to energy sources other than petroleum products and natural gas. It is estimated that over the eight year period from 1978 through 1985, receipts from this tax, net of credits allowed for conversion outlays, will result in over $40 billion in receipts. A substantial share of these general fund receipts will be available to fund the purchase of oil for the Strategic Petroleum Reserve. It will also be available to help finance the credits offered to induce homeowners to make their homes more fuel-efficient, and to finance other conservation incentives.

It is evident, then, that the NEP is a carefully articulated plan in which tax penalties and tax incentives reinforce each other to induce energy conservation and the conversion to energy sources in more ample domestic supply. The revenues arising from some parts of the plan are recycled for other energy-related purposes, with little if any direct net drain on the domestic economy.

I want to turn now to the possible effects of the National Energy Plan on our balance of payments. Currently, our oil bill is dominating the swing in our international trade balance. The trade deficit for the first quarter of the year was almost $7 billion, a significant deterioration from the deficit of $3½ billion in the last quarter of 1976. The first quarter result is more than half attributable to the bulge in oil imports, which totaled over $11 billion for the quarter.

The rising cost and volume of our oil imports is swamping our basically strong position on other parts of our trade picture. We should, of course, be expecting our favorable balance on other trade to diminish at this stage of the business cycle, with recovery returning our imports to more normal levels relative to exports. But rising demands for oil and higher prices charged by foreign oil suppliers have aggravated that decline. As a result, our trade balance, including fuel imports, has moved from a $9 billion surplus in 1975 to a $9 billion deficit in 1976 to a projected deficit this year likely to total over $20 billion. Roughly half of this deterioration is the result of the increase in our bill for imported fuel.

We cannot and should not expect to increase our trade surpluses with other areas of the world so as to offset rising deficits with OPEC countries resulting from our present dependence on oil. Other oil-importing nations are also faced with a large increase in oil import bills and with deficits vis-à-vis OPEC. Any attempt on our part to offset more fully a growing trade deficit with OPEC by increasing our trade surplus with the rest of the world would be almost certain to fail—and to reduce levels of trade and economic output in the process. The additional strain on other countries' external payments as a result of such U.S. actions, would incline them to take counter-measures—either in direct retaliation or by reducing demands for imports from the U.S. by exercising further domestic economic restraint. Either way, the principal result would be a lower level of world output and trade, with equally adverse effects on the U.S. trade balance.

The one way in which we can meaningfully and constructively reduce the U.S. trade deficit is by policies which reduce oil imports. This would benefit not only the U.S. balance of payments, but also aid the balances of other oil consuming nations, particularly the LDC's, by reducing demand pressures on the world price of oil. The President's energy plan will help many countries, and the perception of what it can offer explains the enthusiastic support the President received for it at the Summit meeting last weekend.

In summary, Mr. Chairman, let me acknowledge that there is some price we must all pay to achieve our national and international objectives. But let us not delude ourselves into thinking that other alternatives to the National Energy Plan will cost less. There is one law of economics to which we are all subject. This is the simple precept that "There is no such thing as a free lunch." Do we pay for our lunch in a form of ever-escalating prices for imported oil—a tax levied by foreign suppliers of energy? Do we pass the bill on to those less able to pay, such as the less developed countries? Do we pay for our lunch by passing the bill on to our children? Or do we pay by gradually adjusting our transportation, heating and cooling habits in order to reduce our dependence on foreign suppliers and conserve the dwindling supply of convenient energy resources for future generations? By facing the problem now, when the opportunity exists for gradual adjustments, we buy the time during which accelerated research can open new energy possibilities that will enable us to preserve a standard of living which is the envy of the world.

Statement Prepared for the Joint Economic Committee

ARTHUR B. LAFFER

Arthur B. Laffer's testimony at the Joint Economic Committee hearings on the macroeconomic effect of the National Energy Plan focuses on the disincentives incorporated in the plan in the form of tax increases matched by transfer payments that, he claims, would only reduce output and input growth.

It is again an honor to be invited to appear before this Committee. I, too, share the concerns expressed by the Administration, Congress, and the American people about the problems surrounding energy. The problem is serious, and is increasing in severity. The present time, in my opinion, is the correct time to deal with the problem.

The origins of the current crisis result from both natural and manmade sources. The severity of the current crisis, in my opinion, has primarily come about as a result of poorly conceived policies with predictably bad consequences. As often as not, explicit actions taken to rectify perceived problems exacerbate the problem itself, or cause other problems. I believe the National Energy Plan proposed by the Administration is just such a proposed action. Without exaggeration, the Administration's energy package is the wrong policy at the wrong time.

In a highly simplified form, the National Energy Plan will raise enormous revenues through new and expanded taxes. These receipts will then be put back into the economy in the form of rebates, tax incentives, and transfer payments. A number of economists argue that the destimulative aspects of the higher taxes are offset by the stimulative aspects of the rebates and transfers. They conclude that output or GNP will not be much affected. This is clearly the logic put forth by the Administration.

In my opinion, the above view makes no sense whatsoever. If output resulted solely from aggregate demand, one could construe some logic out of the position. Output, however, results from both aggregate demand and aggregate supply. The above analysis totally ignores aggregate supply and, as such, is completely off the mark. An increase in tax receipts matched by an equal increase in rebates and transfer payments will unambiguously reduce output and output growth. The bigger the tax increase cum rebate, the greater will be the fall in both output and employment.

To see this point clearly, imagine an increase in U.S. taxes of over $1 trillion, matched by an equal rebate right up to the point where workers and producers

Arthur B. Laffer, "Statement Prepared for the Joint Economic Committee hearings on the Macroeconomic Impact of the Administration's National Energy Plan," May 20, 1977. Reprinted by permission.

receive nothing for their work effort, and nonworkers and nonproducers receive everything. Output will fall to zero. While the example is extreme in most instances, the point is clear. Taxes matched by spending reduce output. The Administration's energy package, if put into effect, would raise taxes by an enormous amount annually, and would rebate the proceeds. It would result in an enormous loss in incomes in the country and an enormous loss in employment. Surely at this stage in our history this is not what is needed.

Therefore, if the National Energy Plan as proposed were to become law, it would retard the level of output and economic growth. While its effect would be to reduce net imports of both oil and automobiles, the package would simultaneously increase net imports, or reduce net exports, of other products. The program would add substantially to red tape, filing, and informaton requirements on energy-related firms, while adding little to their domestic production incentives. The major effects of the program will be to discourage energy consumption and production in general.

It is hard to imagine just what groups will benefit from the program. The substantial taxes on gasoline, automobiles, energy production and energy consumption will swamp any benefits conceivable from the rebates. Regionally, Texas, California, and other energy producing areas, as well as car producing centers such as Michigan, Ohio, etc., will be the most damaged.

The rebate aspect of the package has recently shown itself to be an unviable political option as the weak support in the House and, later, the lack of support in the Senate demonstrated.

Here are four key economic aspects of President Carter's proposals:

TAXES

The proposals include a number of significant increases in taxes:

i. On gasoline alone, standby authority is requested to start taxing an additional 5¢ per gallon as of 1/15/78, and rising to 50¢ per gallon by 1985.

ii. Automobiles deemed energy-inefficient by their gas mileage will, starting with the 1978 model line, be taxed up to a maximum of $449. This tax will be increased through the 1985 model line, where the maximum tax will be $2,488.

iii. Domestically produced crude oil will continue indefinitely to be subjected to price ceilings. In addition, three yearly tax increases will be imposed on well-head production until the ceiling price plus tax equals the world price, currently $13.50 per barrel. In the case of old oil, the three-stage tax increase would amount to $8.25 per barrel.

iv. The ceiling price on natural gas sold in interstate markets would be raised to $1.75 per 1000 cubic feet from the current $1.45 price. However, intrastate natural gas, which previously was uncontrolled, will now be subject to the price ceiling.

v. Industrial companies will be taxed at increasing rates on their usage of natural gas. This tax would, under present conditions, start in 1979 at 30¢ per 1000 cubic feet, and rise to $1.10 by 1985. The utility tax on the use of natural gas would commence in 1983, until by 1988 it equalized the energy cost between natural gas and distillate oil. Industrial users of petroleum would be taxed at 90¢ per barrel in 1979, and this would rise to $3.00 per barrel by 1985. Utilities that used petroleum would have a flat tax of $1.50 per barrel, beginning in 1983.

iv. Aviation fuel taxes would be raised 4¢ per gallon, and the rebate of 2¢ per gallon on motorboat fuel would be removed. Efficiency targets on appliances would be made mandatory. The U.S. stockpile of oil would be increased 500 million barrels to 1 billion barrels. Detailed accounting requirements on the energy companies would be imposed and antitrust would be more actively pursued.

However one figures it, the program adds up to a massive increase in overall taxes. Estimates of the ultimate revenue from these tax increases range well over $100 billion per year. When one compares these numbers with the total cost of the Viet Nam war, over a six-year period of, say, $100 billion, one obtains the proper perspective of the proposal's magnitude. As such, the discrepancy between market values and the amounts workers and producers receive would increase dramatically. If ever enacted, this would constitute an enormous increase in the wedge and would lead to sharply curtailed production in the market place. Growth rates would be greatly reduced.

While many of us intuitively think of production distortions in terms of factories, machines, or capital equipment, the effect on individual workers' incentives to work could easily be quite consequential. At an additional tax of 50¢ per gallon, a family that drives 20,000 miles per year in a car that gets 20 miles per gallon, would have an effective reduction in its income of $500. This figure does not even consider the higher price of the car or the plethora of other taxes and their effect on prices. There is a precise equivalence between product taxes and factor taxes. As such, President Carter's program is equivalent to increased income taxes across a broad range of factors from workers, land, on to capital investment itself.

To illustrate the correspondence between product taxes and factor taxes, imagine a person who earns $10,000 gross per year. If he pays a flat 50 percent income tax rate on his earnings, he will be left with $5,000 to spend. If, on the other hand, there is a 50 percent tax on the full sales price of all products, he'll be able to spend $10,000, but the prices of everything will be doubled. In both instances, his after-tax real income is the same. While the exact associations become far more complicated where we include many products and a multitude of factors, the correspondence principle here remains valid.

TRANSFER PAYMENTS

The Administration's program also includes a substantial increase in either explicit or implicit spending:

i. All gasoline taxes and crude oil production taxes will be rebated through the tax system (as credits), and to nontaxpayers. These rebates, in part, will be biased toward home-heating oil buyers.

ii. Automobiles attaining a specified degree of fuel efficiency will be eligible for rebates up to $473 maximum for 1978 model cars, and increasing over time to $493 for 1985 model cars.

iii. Firms purchasing equipment to generate electricity would receive a 10 percent tax credit on the purchase price.

iv. Homeowners would receive a tax credit not to exceed $2,000 for investment in solar equipment. Businesses would receive a 10 percent tax credit on solar equipment.

Virtually all of the revenues from the increased taxes would go toward increased government spending, thus mitigating any chances of offsetting tax reductions or reduced national debt. This part of the Carter program merely consummates the additions to the overall tax wedge. Whereas tax increases in one area, resulting in tax reductions elsewhere, may lead to expanded output, tax increases matched by transfer spending increases will only reduce output and output growth. Overall, the fundamental form of taxation is government spending irrespective of financing technique used.

TARIFF AND TRADE

In his proposal to tax the purchase price of low-gas efficiency cars and give rebates to high-gas efficiency cars, there was an explicit exclusion of non-American and non-Canadian made cars. The actual treatment of these foreign cars is to be determined by direct negotiation. This differential treatment of foreign versus domestic made cars is equivalent to a tariff on foreign made automobiles. Imports of automobiles will be retarded.

The tax increase and rebate aspects of the energy program will also have two effects that will impact on international trade. First, the tax increases will thwart domestic consumption of energy relative to domestic production. Energy imports should fall. Second, the general increase in taxes and transfers will restrict the overall domestic supply of output. Such a supply shift will tend to increase total imports relative to exports. Therefore, the U.S. trade balance will be adversely impacted by the program.

With a deteriorating trade balance combined with reduced net imports of both energy and automobiles, there should be an increase in the net imports, or a reduction in the net exports of other products. These changes should be more than sufficient to offset any improvements in the energy and automobile accounts.

TAX INCIDENCE AND TOTAL REVENUE

While the precise incidence of the President's heightened tax and spending programs is not known, it is clear they do increase the progressivity of the federal government's impact on the economy. The increased taxes on big cars, the numerous business taxes, the specific limitations on tax credits, the overall bias against energy usage (assumed by most economists as a "luxury" good), and the egalitarian tendency of the rebates, unambiguously raises the incidence of the tax structure on upper income groups relative to middle and lower income groups. All groups, nonetheless, will experience an increased tax incidence, albeit greater for upper income groups. Whatever one's perception of the fairness or equity value of such a move, such a redistribution of the tax incidence will lower output even further.

Often it is the case that the incidence of a tax is very different from the burden of a tax. Raising tax rates on upper income and wealthy people may actually have the effect of lowering the after-tax incomes of the poor and working class people. Given the level of spending in New York City, if the City were to tax all incomes over $100,000 per year at a 100 percent tax rate, it is clear that they would get next to nothing in revenues. Those people with incomes in excess of $100,000 per year would either move, or find ways to not report the excess. Given the need to finance the spending, taxes, either explicit or implicit, on lower incomes would have to rise. Therefore, by lowering tax rates on upper income groups, the burden of the tax on lower income groups may actually be reduced. I believe we are well within this range at present. Any increase in the progressive incidence of taxation actually places a heavier burden on the poor and low-income people.

It is not only conceivable but quite possible, that the entire program will, when combined with existing taxes and spending programs, lead to reduced overall revenue and markedly higher spending. Deficits will most likely be increased as a result of the overall program. When one thinks that reductions in output lead to a reduction in other tax receipts, increased spending on such programs as unemployment compensation, Social Security, etc., it is hard to imagine anything other than expanded federal deficits. The increased burden on our State and local governments could be substantial.

OTHER CONSIDERATIONS

As a final analytic point on the overall effects of President Carter's energy package, it would tend to strengthen the OPEC oil cartel. A major influence leading to the historical dissolution of cartels has been the market responses to abnormal pricing structures. If a cartel sets its price too high not only will consumption tend to fall, but also producers will invariably face supply prices that are highly profitable on the margin. These production "incentives" entice suppliers to either violate the cartel quantity restrictions or induce new producers to enter production.

The recent energy proposal virtually eliminates the producers' incentives to break down the cartel. As the formulae go, increases in the world price of oil will be matched one for one by increases in the tax on oil production. Thus, in the event of a price increase in world markets, U.S. producers of oil will not receive any higher prices. There will not be any added incentives to produce. This avenue of offset to any OPEC oil price increase will be closed by explicit government policy.

As a final point, I would add that virtually every objective of the Administration's proposal would be better served by the immediate decontrol of energy with a standby excess profits tax authority over a two-year horizon.

Freedom for Fuel?

LOS ANGELES TIMES

The issue of decontrol of oil and gas producers has been heavily debated during the time that national attention has been focused on energy. The following article discusses the possible hazards of decontrol and the characteristics of the National Energy Plan that its supporters contend make it the more desirable route to take.

If Congress approves President Carter's energy plan, Americans will be paying more for fuels. But, initially at least, most of that extra money will go to the government in the form of taxes instead of to oil and gas producers in the form of profits.

That has left the oil and gas people unhappy, though given what Carter wants to accomplish—a slowdown in energy demand—and what he wants to avoid—a major inflationary impact—we think it makes sense.

What the oil and gas industries want is for the government to drop its controls on prices they can charge for their products. Let prices on domestic fuels rise to the world level, they argue, and profits will be generated that will allow major investment in finding and developing new oil and gas resources. In other words, let there be a free market in energy and the supply problem will take care of itself.

The trouble with this argument is that it assumes a number of things that are far from certain.

Timing is one. Most unexploited reserves of oil and gas lie offshore, on the outer continental shelf. Could the difficult job of finding, extracting and processing these fuels in amounts adequate to national needs and under environmentally acceptable conditions take place quickly enough to avoid the energy crunch that looms for the early 1980s? The doubt about that is enormous.

Levels of investment are a second uncertainty. Would higher profits translate into greatly expanded exploration, drilling, refining and whatever, or might a good part of those profits go into nonenergy areas—real estate, department stores, metals and the like—as oil companies pursued their interests in diversification? Our only guide here is experience, and experience has already shown that profits derived from oil are not necessarily reinvested in oil.

Finally, there is the inflationary effect of immediate decontrol. In gasoline prices alone, each 1-cent-a-gallon increase at current rates of consumption means $1.1 billion a year more out of consumers' pockets. If domestic oil jumped to the world price, gasoline would cost 7 cents a gallon more, and all other petroleum products would rise commensurately. The public would pay heavily for that, in dollars and jobs.

The Carter energy plan seeks to avoid these hazards. It would give development incentives to oil and gas producers by allowing newly discovered oil to be priced at world levels, and gas at prices far higher than those now permitted. It would dampen fuel demand by imposing wellhead taxes to raise prices of oil and gas to so-called "replacement" cost levels. But the inflationary impact of these higher prices would be offset by returning the taxes to consumers in other forms.

The Carter policy recognizes that it is far cheaper to conserve a barrel of oil—it costs about $3.50 to do that—than it is to produce a new barrel, which costs about $13.50. It recognizes that decontrol of prices likely would lead not only to massive windfall profits but also to speeded-up depletion of existing U.S. reserves, with no assurance that sufficient new oil discoveries would be found.

Those who doubt this might recall some recent history. From the late 1950s to the early 1970s, the U.S. government—at the behest of some of the same domestic oil producers who want a "free market" now—imposed severe quotas on imported oil. The purpose was to keep out cheap crude and, in so doing, to increase the demand for the higher-priced U.S. product. The result was to accelerate the depletion of American oil reserves. And that, of course, has helped put us in the fix we are in today.

Energy Issue Puts Squeeze Play on Carter

ERNEST CONINE

Ernest Conine, *Los Angeles Times* editorial writer, comments on the inequities, both regional and individual, in Carter's National Energy Plan. He views the higher gasoline taxes as constituting the biggest hurdle standing in the way of public and congressional approval of the plan.

With the best will in the world, President Carter is going to have a very tough time delivering on his promise that his far-reaching energy program will be fair—that it will demand "equal sacrifices from every region, every class of people, every interest group."

It is extremely important, of course, for him to try—and be seen by the people as trying—to translate this promise into reality.

The American people have demonstrated that they are capable of great sacrifice—far more than would be required of them by the President's energy program. But they must be persuaded, first, that the sacrifice is really necessary and, second, that the burden is fairly shared.

In the case of Carter's energy program, meeting the first imperative is hard enough. Many, many people still prefer to believe that the energy crisis is a sham. And Congress, unfortunately, has an oversupply of nonstatesmen who would rather nurture illusion than confront reality.

The President, however, will find it even harder to deliver on his equality-of-sacrifice promise. For example:

A 5-cents-a-gallon increase in gasoline prices requires far less sacrifice from a New York secretary who commutes to work on the train than from a Californian who lives in Pacoima and drives 20 miles to and from work every day.

High utility bills will, by their nature, hurt the poor but not the rich. It's easier for the fellow with a 10-room house and a heated swimming pool to adjust by using less gas and electricity than for the little old lady who lives in a one-room apartment. And whereas the affluent can take advantage of tax credits to buy energy-saving home insulation or solar heating units, the not-so-affluent simply don't have the money for such investments.

There are bound to be regional inequities, too.

For many Americans who live east of the Mississippi River, an automobile is a luxury, for most Americans in the West and Southwest, it is a necessity.

The auto worker in Michigan or Georgia or California faces the risk, under the President's plan, of being hit twice. He not only would have to pay higher fuel prices the same as everybody else, but if the tax on gas-guzzlers caused a falloff in auto sales, he might lose his job as well.

The same is true of people whose livelihoods depend upon the American yen

Ernest Conine, "Energy Issue Puts Squeeze Play on Carter," *Los Angeles Times*, April 25, 1977, Part II, p. 7. Copyright, 1977, Los Angeles Times. Reprinted by permission.

for the open road; if higher energy prices achieve their conservation purpose, there will be fewer travelers spending money at motels, roadside restaurants, ski lodges and fishing resorts.

The Carter plan seeks to ease the pain by providing, in effect, for returning with one hand the money it takes from people in higher fuel taxes with the other.

The details still aren't clear. But the general idea is to maintain consumer buying power—and therefore alleviate individual hardships and avoid setting off a new recession—by returning all the money collected in fuel taxes to the economy through some combination of income-tax reductions, special payments and other steps.

A key factor in the Carter plan is that the size of the tax deduction or payment would bear no relation to the amount of fuel taxes a particular person has paid. This means that the fellow who held down his energy consumption could actually come out ahead, while the citizen who didn't might not get enough back from the government to pay his higher fuel and utility bills.

Such a system, if enacted, will go a long way toward preventing undue hardship for low-income Americans. But it won't remove inequities; those individuals and regions which depend least on the automobile will still come out better than those where distances are long and public transportation is sparse or unavailable.

Perfect justice is not attainable, of course, in an imperfect world. The amount of sacrifice required by the President's proposal is not all that great in any event, nor are the inequalities of sacrifice all that serious.

To some extent, inequities would balance out. Californians would sacrifice more in higher gasoline bills, but Easterners would make their sacrifice in terms of higher heating bills.

Beyond that, the impact would be spread over a perid of time, giving us time to adjust.

The tax on gas-guzzling cars would be imposed in steps, giving the automakers time to adjust their production and marketing systems to the emphasis on smaller cars.

Higher gasoline taxes would not begin before January, 1979—and would not be imposed then or later if fuel conservation goals were met. And while these taxes would hurt some people more than others, an intelligent system of recycling the money back to consumers would mean that very few people, poor or otherwise, would suffer genuine hardship.

But the initial congressional reaction suggests that the President is going to find it very dificult to win approval for the gasoline tax portion of his plan. The danger is that in the name of correcting regional and other inequities, Congress will grant so many exceptions that the legislation will become a meaningless mishmash. Or, resistance to the gasoline tax increase may cause harmful delays in the whole program.

Carter might do himself and his program a favor by reconsidering whether sharply higher gasoline taxes will really produce enough dividends in conservation to make up for the problems—political and otherwise—which they raise.

Gasoline consumption by automobiles, after all, accounts for only about 12% of U.S. energy use; the biggest potential for conservation lies in fuel and power consumption by business and industry.

To the degree that gasoline conservation is feasible, the combination of penalty taxes on purchase of gas-guzzling cars and rebates for purchase of energy-efficient vehicles is likely to be far more effective than higher gasoline taxes anyway.

But while Congress has the right and the duty to make constructive changes in Carter's program, it will do the American people a serious disservice if it fails to enact legislation which will substantially meet the goals set by the President.

We live in a world where oil and gas reserves are being used up faster than new energy supplies can be developed; we have no choice but to curtail our energy consumption. The only question is whether we begin to do it now, while there is still time for only moderately painful adjustments, or wait until it's too late to avoid the "catastrophe" of which the President warned.

If we choose the latter course, the question of "equal sacrifice" will be the least of our worries.

4/
THE STEIGER-HANSEN BILL

Tax reform legislation in 1969 and 1976 limited the use of tax "loopholes" and the benefits from tax preferences. Since that time, the maximum capital gains tax rate has gone from 25 percent to 49.1 percent. This increase in the tax rate on capital gains has effectively narrowed the difference between the after-tax return on ordinary income and on capital gains, obviously making individual investment in equities less attractive.

In response to the claimed disincentives embodied in the present capital gains tax structure, the Investment Incentive Act of 1978—or the Steiger-Hansen bill—was introduced and served to initiate the debate on capital gains. The bill seeks to roll back the maximum tax rate on capital gains for individuals and corporations to its pre-1969 level of 25 percent. Capital gains would no longer be subject to the minimum tax on excessive preferences. It would also be removed as a preference item that offsets the amount of wages eligible for the preference limiting the maximum tax on wages and salaries to a 50 percent ceiling.

The federal tax structure is believed by Steiger supporters to be a major factor impeding capital formation by favoring consumption and discouraging saving and investment. A cut in the capital gains tax rate is seen as a potential boost to job creation, productivity, and economic growth. The capital gains tax is considered a mechanism that "locks in" investors by reducing the incentive to invest and by increasing its cost. It also inhibits the free flow of resources in the equity market. One of the strongest arguments in favor of capital gains tax cuts is the current common practice of paying taxes on "paper gains" caused by inflation.

Opponents of the Steiger-Hansen bill criticize its inequitable treatment of various taxpaying groups by taxing capital gains at a lower rate than ordinary income and by reducing the rates on higher-income individuals rather than the middle- and lower-income taxpayers. Another concern is the loss of tax revenues to the federal government, which they presume will result.

In the subsequent pages, some congressional testimonies and commentary are offered to further clarify the favorable aspects and criticisms of the Steiger-Hansen bill.

Statement Before the Subcommittee on Taxation and Debt Management

OTTO ECKSTEIN

The trade-off between stimulating capital formation and fairly distributing income and wealth is treated in the following testimony on capital gains tax bills by Otto Eckstein, president of Data Resources, Inc., before the Senate Finance Committee's Subcommittee on Taxation and Debt Management. One of his suggestions for assisting low-to-middle income taxpayers is to reduce the taxation of the inflation component of capital gains.

The question of capital gains taxation is one of the most difficult in terms of economic structure and performance. Issues of capital information and competition quickly run up against issues of taxpayer equity and social justice. The long-term development strategy for the American economy—just how we intend to accomplish the necessary process of innovation and capital information—is at stake in the current debate.

CAPITAL GAINS AND TAX REFORM

Ever since personal income tax rates were boosted to their modern peak levels in World War II, preferential capital gains rates have been the central feature of the tax code which brought down the effective tax rates for middle and high income individuals, and have therefore been at the center of the struggle for tax reform. Quite apart from their relation to normal capital gains realized on common stock, real estate and homes, the capital gains rates are an essential part of various tax shelters, many of which consisted, essentially, in transforming ordinary income into capital gains.

The tax reform movement got nowhere from World War II until the Nixon presidency, when the public became thoroughly aroused and the political impasse in the Congress was broken. As a result, major tax reform legislation was passed in 1969 and 1976, closing much of the capital gains "loophole" and reducing the benefits of the associated tax shelters. As a result, the maximum rate of taxation on capital gains increased from 25 to 49.1%. State and local income taxes also rose sharply during this period. The President's 1978 tax proposals would have pursued this line of reform further, aiming to bring the Federal maximum rate on capital gains to 52.5%, and the aggregate rate in the typical industrial state close to 60%.

Otto Eckstein, statement in *Special Supplement: Statements at Hearing by Subcommittee on Taxation and Debt Management of Senate Finance Committee on Capital Gains Tax Bills* (Washington, D.C.: The Bureau of National Affairs, Inc., June 29, 1978). Reprinted by permission of The Bureau of National Affairs, Inc.

WHAT WENT WRONG?

Instead of providing general satisfaction, the reform of capital gains taxation has increasingly raised questions which have now brought us to a point where this trend is likely to be reversed. The surprises have included the following quote:

1. *Inflation became severe.* It was always recognized that inflation-created increases in nominal values of capital assets should not be taxed. When inflation averaged 1.9% as it did from 1952 to 1969, and the rate of increase of stock prices was 8.5%, the inaccuracy of taxing capital gains without inflation adjustment was a minor matter more than offset by the exclusion of half of capital gains from the tax base.[1]

But inflation since 1969 has averaged 6.5%, and the stock market has failed to rise at all, so the effective capital gains tax burden has become confiscatory in many circumstances. . . . In nominal terms, the stock market peaked in 1968 and then began to oscillate in a horizontal band; in real terms, deflating the stock price index by the consumer price index, the peak is seen in 1965 with fluctuations about a downtrend thereafter.

Furthermore, the protection of capital for middle income families against inflation has proved particularly difficult, and the government has chosen not to offer any vehicle to make it easier.

2. *The stock market acted badly after the capital gains reforms and dried up as a source of capital.* To be sure, the worsening economic environment was the principal factor in the dramatic downward revaluation of earnings. Inflation brought high interest rates and lower multiples. But the increase in taxation was also a major factor.

For the typical individual in income brackets that are affected by the post-1968 tax reforms, the stock market became a "tails-you-win, heads-I-lose" proposition with real gains taxed more heavily and loss offset severely limited. Institutional investors which pay no tax became the principal actors in the stock market.

The decline in the stock market was particularly important to new and smaller companies. Many large companies do not issue stock beyond the modest sales through stock option and employee purchase plans. The utility industry, always the biggest issuer of stock, has regulated prices and so, within limits, is able to pass the high cost of equity capital forward to the consumer. But the stock market is of importance for new companies and to those growing particularly rapidly.

The virtual disappearance of the "new issues" market during the 1970s has meant that this avenue for financing new enterprises has been virtually closed. Since these units are the source of much of our technoogical progress, this is a serious loss to economic development. Large institutions managing pension

[1]Roger Brinner, "Inflation and the Definition of Taxable Personal Income," in *Inflation and the Income Tax*, ed. by Henry Aaron, The Brookings Institution, 1976; and R. Brinner, "Inflation, Deferral and the Neutral Taxation of Capital Gains," *National Tax Journal*, December 1973.

funds have no interest in small new enterprises, and even if they did, ERISA [Employee Retirement Income Security Act] would make them supercautious.

3. *The rate of capital formation fell sharply, to inadequate levels.* There are many reasons for the drop in investment. The business cycles became more volatile and the utilization rate of industry has been at abnormally low levels since 1973. The profit share and the rate of return on capital have fallen, largely as a result. The expectations of future output reflect a lessened degree of optimism, and consequently companies have marked down their long-run capital expansion plans. But the cost of capital has also been an important element in creating the low-investment situation.

Debt capital, corrected for inflation, has not been expensive nor has it been scarce since the credit crunches of 1973–74. But equity capital, which for many companies is an essential ingredient to external financing in order to hold down the degree of leverage of their balance sheets, has been very difficult to accomplish and has been very costly. The volume of new issues has fallen sharply. The present earnings multiple on stocks as a whole has fallen very sharply . . . and the multiples on smaller, higher risk companies are down a lot more.

DOES THE STOCK MARKET MATTER?

The accumulating research of the 1960's and 1970's points quite strongly toward important effects of stock market behavior on the economy.[2,3] Reflecting the general body of research as well as our own work, the DRI model of the U.S. economy has the following principal channels from the stock market to general economic performance.

1. It is an important determinant of the cost of capital which enters into business fixed investment decisions;

2. It is a large and volatile component of household financial assets, and thereby substantially affects consumer spending;

3. It affects a choice in the portfolio decisions between bonds and stocks.

The stock market affects the economy in many other ways that are difficult to model. For example, we have seen in recent years that its behavior determines the attractiveness of foreign financial investment in the United States, and that a rising stock market strengthens the dollar and reduces inflation. Equally important, it affects the rate of technological progress through its provision of venture capital to innovative enterprises.

Finally, the stock market affects the degree of concentration of the economy: a broad stockmarket facilitates capital formation by smaller com-

---

[2]For example, see 1) Barry Bosworth, "The Stock Market and the Economy," *Brookings Paper on Economic Activity*, 1975:2; 2) *Consumer Spending and Monetary Policy: The Linkages*, Federal Reserve Bank of Boston, 1971;

[3]John J. Arena, "Postwar Stock Market Changes and Consumer Spending," *Review of Economics and Statistics*, November 1965, and the many other references cited in these studies.

panies; an excessive stock market creates a wave of mergers and monop-
olization.

DOES CAPITAL GAINS TAXATION AFFECT THE STOCK MARKET?

The behavior of the stock market has defied much logical analysis. In the absence of a generally accepted quantitative model of behavior, it is impossible to
achieve definitive answers to the impact of any policy move—or of anything
else—on the stock market.

While there is no precise theory, there are some generally agreed upon ideas
with which virtually any serious student of the subject would agree.

The behavior of the stock market depends upon (1) the expected future path
of earnings and/or dividends; (2) interest rates to discount the future earnings/
dividends streams; (3) the riskiness of the returns; (4) the returns and riskiness
of alternative investments; (5) expectations about the economic and political
environment and a model of their relation to returns and their valuation; (6)
internal, technical factors in the market which may accentuate price swings;
and (7) the tax structures, now and expected for the future, which apply to the
principal participants in the market.

The potential importance of the tax factor in the stock market cannot be
assessed precisely, but some general quantitative magnitudes can be identified.
Over intervals as long as several decades, nominal capital gains represent about
half of the total nominal return on common stocks. Therefore as an outer limit, a
universal capital gains tax of 50% could lower the after tax return by as much as
25%. However, the impact must be scaled down substantially for several
factors.

First, many of the institutional participants in the stock market, typified by
the pension funds and some insurance reserves, are not taxable, while others
such as individual Keogh plans and IRA's, are not taxable until the owner has
retired and is in a lower tax bracket. Because of the existence of capital gains
taxation at meaningful levels since 1941 and rapidly rising levels since 1969, the
share of stocks held by nontaxable entities has risen sharply, of course. At this
time, about 25% of stocks are held by them, and of the taxable holdings, a
substantial percentage is not traded.[4]

Second, while stock ownership is highly concentrated, about 40% of all
individually held stocks are in the hands of families that are not in the 50+9%
tax brackets, and whose capital gains tax therefore is below 25%.[5] A crude
calculation of the distribution of common stock holdings by income class
suggests that the average effective tax rate, at the margin on capital gains, is
approximately 25%.

Finally, because the tax is levied only upon the realization of capital gains,

---

[4]Estimate based on the 1971 distribution of dividends to tax-exempt entities reported in
Marshall E. Blume et al., "Stock Ownership in the United States: Characteristics and
Trends," *Survey of Current Business*, November 1974.

[5]Blume, et al., estimate that tax paying units with a 1971 adjusted gross income (AGI) of
$25,000 or less controlled 40.2% of the market value of all stocks. A $25,000 AGI implies a
marginal tax rate equal to or slightly below 50%.

the average effective rate is reduced through delay and, even after the important tax reforms of 1976, through partial escape at death.

The combined impact of delay, current rates less than the 49.1% maximum and substantial tax-exempt ownership is an effective marginal rate for all participants averaging only 14%.[6]

A ceiling rate of 25% on realized gains would only reduce this effective rate by 2.7% to 11.3%. This translates into a 3% increase in shareholder income (net gains plus net dividends), and a "rational" long-run stock market response would be of the same order of magnitude, though perhaps slightly higher to reflect feedback effects of the fiscal stimulus.

Even if one had confidence in the precision of the stock market response estimate (e.g., the 3% just cited), tax receipt estimates would still be precarious. Revenue effects are particularly difficult to calculate because the tax affects the public's willingness to realize capital gains. The amount of realizations incurred by individuals in the upper capital gains tax brackets is extremely small, so that the principal effect of the current tax is not to raise revenue but to reduce realizations. To the extent the lock-in effect is reduced, greater revenue will be received by the Treasury.

ECONOMETRIC MODEL ANALYSIS
UNDER VARIOUS STOCK MARKET ASSUMPTIONS

To cast some light on the impact of a reduction in capital gains taxes on the economy, a series of simulations have been run with the DRI model under alternative stock market assumptions. The capital gains tax reduction, assuming realizations to be unaffected, is assumed to be equal to $2 billion, about the magnitude of some of the current proposals.

Some 50% of this reduction is assumed to benefit owners of common stock, directly through changes in personal taxes and indirectly through changes in corporate gains taxes.

If the reform focuses on fuller capital gains tax relief for homeowners or real estate investments, some of the economic effects of the solution would not materialize, particularly those aiding business fixed investment. On the other hand, construction demand would presumably strengthen.

A $2 billion reduction in capital gains taxation would represent a 20%–25% reduction in the total gains tax. Table 1 summarizes the economy-wide results under various assumptions about the stock market.[7] In the most favorable case, where the stock market rises by a full 10% after one year in response to the tax move, business fixed investment would be boosted by 2.6% by the third year, consumer spending would be up 0.7% in response to the greater house-

---

[6] 14%=26.3% average marginal rate on gains where realized,

  x .70 reduction in implicit tax due to delay

  x .75 share held by taxable units.

[7] The central case (Case 2) is based on a "purely rational" response of the market to the change in aftertax profits, which we estimate will rise 3.6% in response to a change such as is embodied in Steiger-Hansen legislation. The dividend payout ratio is adjusted by 4% to reflect the estimated change in the opportunity cost of dividends relative to retained earnings from the shareholder's perspective. The other cases reflect hypothetical, "emotional" over- or under-reaction to the tax change.

hold wealth and the stronger economy, and unemployment would be reduced by 0.2%.

On the other hand, there would be some crowding out of housing activity. The Federal deficit would not be significantly affected because a stronger economy would bring in additional revenue to offset the initial loss while simultaneously raising the cost of Federal purchases and interest payments.

The macroeconomic effects of a limited change in capital gains taxation are themselves of a rather small order of magnitude. If the only goal is to stimulate investment as a whole, about equally good, perhaps even slightly better results can be achieved by the traditional tax incentives of ever more liberal depreciation allowances and larger investment tax credits.

The issue of capital gains tax relief, therefore, is not primarily a question of macroeconomic effects in the short or intermediate term. The issues are really of two sorts: first, taxpayer equity, income and wealth distribution, second, the strategy of capital formation in the evolution of the economy's industrial structure.

THE QUESTION OF INCOME DISTRIBUTION

While the increases in capital gains taxation of 1969 and 1976 principally affected the high income taxpayers, this is not sufficient reason to impose the same distributional pattern in reverse if some tax relief is to be granted. The injustice growing out of the accelerated inflation is an important factor to be considered.

Consequently, from the point of view of taxpayer equity and income distribution, a capital gains tax reduction program should include a reduction of taxation of the inflation component of capital gains.

The inflation distortion of nominal capital income is greatest for low-to-middle income groups. In the area of corporate securities, high income groups have typically invested in low-payout, rapid-appreciation stocks, so that the illusory inflation share of their gains has been relatively small. In contrast, low-to-middle income taxpayers have not been able to shield their investments against inflation: their "gains" on corporate stocks and other securities largely vanish after adjusting the purchase price of their assets for the inflation which occurs between time of purchase and time of sale . . .

Similar results are obtained for capital gains on residences and other real estate. The 1962 data indicated that the lower income groups actually suffer losses on an inflation-adjusted basis, while the well-to-do lost only approximately one quarter of their apparent gains to inflation.[8] The stronger housing market of recent years may have improved the picture for the middle class.

Of course, this strength is itself principally due to the desperate effort of many Americans to protect their savings—a transition of American attitudes to treat housing as a hedge against inflation. In effect, for most middle-class families, owning a home has been the only effective means of protecting their savings. Yet when those homes are sold, the "roll-over" provisions that are open to them require home-ownership until death, which is impossible for many older people as their incomes and their ability to manage separate households dwindle.

[8]Brinner, "Inflation and the Definition of Taxable Personal Income."

TABLE 1
The Macroeconomic and Budgetary Impacts
of a $2 Billion Reduction in Capital Gains Taxation

ECONOMIC IMPACT (Percentage change from baseline)

	1979	1980	1981	1982	1983
Average Common Stock Price					
Case 1	0.7	1.0	0.8	0.6	0.6
Case 2	2.9	3.9	3.7	3.1	2.8
Case 3	7.1	9.7	9.2	8.1	7.5
Gross National Product (At 1972 prices)					
Case 1	0.1	0.1	0.1	0.1	0.1
Case 2	0.1	0.3	0.4	0.3	0.3
Case 3	0.1	0.5	0.7	0.6	0.5
Unemployment Rate					
Case 1	−0.0	−0.0	−0.1	−0.0	−0.0
Case 2	−0.0	−0.1	−0.1	−0.1	−0.1
Case 3	−0.0	−0.2	−0.2	−0.2	−0.1
Consumer Spending (At 1972 prices)					
Case 1	0.1	0.2	0.2	0.2	0.2
Case 2	0.1	0.3	0.4	0.4	0.4
Case 3	0.2	0.6	0.7	0.8	0.8
Business Fixed Investment (At 1972 prices)					
Case 1	0.1	0.3	0.4	0.4	0.3
Case 2	0.1	0.7	1.3	1.5	1.5
Case 3	0.2	1.4	2.6	2.8	2.3

BUDGETARY IMPACT (Change relative to baseline, $ billions)

	1979	1980	1981	1982	1983
Federal Surplus					
Case 1	−1.5	−1.3	−1.3	−1.7	−2.2
Case 2	−1.4	−0.2	0.5	0.0	−0.8
Case 3	−1.0	1.9	3.7	2.8	1.1
Federal Receipts					
Case 1	−1.5	−1.1	−0.8	−0.7	−0.6
Case 2	−1.4	−0.0	1.3	2.0	2.4
Case 3	−1.0	2.2	5.2	6.4	7.0

The impact is quite sensitive to the estimated stock market response and the corresponding impacts on capital costs and household wealth. Three cases were evaluated:

CASE 1: 1% near-term increase in the stock market, 1% reduction in dividends
CASE 2: 4% near-term increase in the stock market, 4% reduction in dividends
CASE 3: 10% near-term increase in the stock market, 10% reduction in dividends

The stock market changes were phased in over one year, the dividend changes over four years.

The simplest measure to help middle-class families would be to relieve them of capital gains tax on the residences even if there is no "roll-over" into a new residence. A more general relief measure would introduce an inflation step-up of the capital gains basis for tax purposes, a step-up which could be applied to all tax entities, perhaps only to certain portions, perhaps only partially. The weakness of this approach is that a similar correction is equally justifiable for the net interest received or paid on other assets and liabilities.

In summary, the proposals now most widely discussed, introduced by Congressmen Steiger and Jones and by Senator Hansen, focus too much of the attention on undoing the increases of 1969 and 1976, and do not deal sufficiently with the urgent and substantial problem of capital gains relief for middle income taxpayers who are particularly hurt by capital gains taxes applied to value changes created by inflation.

WHAT STRATEGY FOR CAPITAL FORMATION?

The proposals to reduce capital gains taxation must be partly viewed as one particular strategy for improving the country's rate of capital formation. Ever since 1954, tax policy has encouraged the retention of earnings, particularly by large, capital-intensive corporations.

. . . The principal tax changes have, with few exceptions, been favorable to capital formation within corporations, and unfavorable to capital formation that has to pass the test of the market. President Eisenhower liberalized depreciation practices. President Kennedy instituted the investment tax credit and liberalized depreciation once more. President Johnson reduced both personal and corporate tax rates, the only measure that can be interpreted as having at least one favorable component to market-based capital formation.

In the Nixon-Ford years, depreciation was liberalized once more, the investment credit was made more generous, while the major tax reforms of 1969 and 1975 were enacted to greatly increase the taxation of individual return on capital.

The repeated encouragement of earnings retention was of major benefit to capital formation. The preponderant body of scientific opinion accepts the effectiveness of such tax incentive measures as investment credits and depreciation allowances. This viewpoint is reflected in President Carter's proposals to apply the investment credit to industrial buildings and to the proposed corporate rate reduction.

However, unending pursuit of the earnings retention strategy gradually does change the pattern of capital formation. While the average effective rate of corporate taxation has fallen from 44.5% in 1951 to approximately 30% today,[9] the cost of externally obtained equity capital has become very high due to the stock market decline, and the availability of equity capital to new and smaller enterprises has been virtually lost.

In the long run, this one-sided strategy creates an economy dominated by large, well-established enterprises, whose managements are little dependent upon their stockholders or on sources of external debt capital. A shrinking proportion of all investment is required to pass the test of the capital market, as we rely increasingly on the plowing back of the retained earnings and depreciation flows.

If a step up in capital formation is accepted as a goal of policy—and I am aware of few observers who do not accept that premise—then there is a strong

[9]Joseph A. Pechman, *Federal Tax Policy*, The Brookings Institution, 1977, page 138.

case that at least a portion of the tax resources to be devoted to that purpose be flowed through the market channel, rather than exclusively poured once more into retained earnings.

The results will be difficult to assess econometrically because there has been so little experience with the market approach. But the poor behavior of the stock market since 1969 and the virtual disappearance of new common stock issues to help the smaller and newer enterprise are pretty strong evidence that increases in these taxes had a significant negative effect, and therefore raise a realistic promise that reductions in these taxes would be comparably helpful.

CONCLUSION

There is a good case for some reduction in capital gains taxation. It could be the beginning of a market-based strategy of aiding capital formation. It would also be a recognition that the recent inflation has made a portion of capital gains illusory, and therefore properly subject to some tax relief.

The exact form of the capital gains tax relief is a more difficult issue. The Steiger-Jones-Hansen proposals would limit the reductions almost entirely to the high income individuals who were affected by the tax reforms of 1969 and 1975. Capital gains relief should be applied to a broader segment of the capital-owning public.

A more equitable capital gains package would include a change in the treatment of a family's home, perhaps terminating its capital gains taxation altogether. A broader reduction in capital gains taxation that would enhance the fairness of the tax system woul allow an inflation adjustment on the basis of property for the tax, thereby limiting the tax to real increases in value.

The administration of an inflation adjustment would be relatively simple, requiring only the addition of one easily calculated column on the capital gains tax form and a simple table of inflation factors.

The proposed method of dealing with the inflation distortion of capital gains by writing-up the purchase price of capital assets is decidedly superior to the alternatives, mechanically changing the share of the gain included in AGI as the holding period increases.

A graduated, rising exclusion, in fact, runs counter to the logic of adjustment for inflation. For example, it should be clear that the relatively high consumer price inflation and low stock price growth in recent years indicate that most appreciation in recently purchased shares is illusory, whereas long-held assets reflect substantial real increases. Related inflation adjustments could also be extended to savings accounts and other assets generating ordinary income and, on the reverse side, to interest payments by consumers and business.

The proposals now before the Congress pose the conflict between the question of capital formation and the question of a fair distribution of income and wealth too strongly. There are better proposals, and we would urge both the Administration and the Congress to come forth with them.

Economic and Investment Observations: Capital Gains Tax Rate Reduction

ARTHUR B. LAFFER

The suggestion that a reduction of high marginal tax rates may stimulate economic activity and increase tax revenues has advanced rapidly during recent months to the forefront of economic discussion. Arthur D. Laffer's testimony before the Senate Finance Committee's Subcommittee on Taxation and Debt Management on June 29, 1978, stresses the direct impact a capital gains tax cut would have on investment incentives and capital mobility.

Reduction of the tax rates on capital gains is an integral part of much needed tax reform. Over the last decade, U.S. real economic growth has been far too slow. Needed social programs have been postponed or diverted into stopgap welfare plans which can only attempt to temper the effects of high unemployment rates, reduced after-tax incomes and generally poor economic performance.

The most debilitating act a government can perpetrate on its citizens is to adopt policies that destroy the economy's production base, for it is the production base that generates any prosperity to be found in the society. U.S. tax policies over the last decade have had the effect of damaging this base by removing many of the incentives to economic advancement. It is necessary to restore those incentives if we are to cure our economic palsy.

The resources spent by the government come from the total tax burden on the economy's productive sector. Whether government spending translates into public services, transfer payments or pure waste, government resources must come from the economy's workers and producers. As such, these resources comprise a major part of the wedge driven between the payments made for factor services and the payment received by the factors themselves. Increases in this wedge, taken alone, raise wages paid for factor services, lower wages received by the factors themselves, and thereby lower the demand for and the supply of productive factor inputs. As a consequence, output falls.

A reduction in capital gains tax rates does nothing *directly* to impact this aggregate wedge. To stop at this apparent conclusion, however, would miss not only the essence of the proposals to reduce these tax rates, but many of the lessons from the history of taxation as well.

Output depends as much on an individual factor's tax rates as it does on the overall tax burden. If one productive factor is faced with exceptionally burdensome tax rates, it will withdraw from the marketplace. Its departure will lower

Arthur B. Laffer, *"Economic and Investment Observations: Capital Gains Tax Rate Reduction* (Boston: H.C. Wainwright & Co., August 1, 1978). Reprinted by permission of H.C. Wainwright & Co.

output by its production potential and, in turn, reduce the production potential of all other factors with which it is complementary.

For example, high productivity and high wages for truck drivers require the existence of trucks to drive. If trucks are taxed excessively, there simply won't be as many trucks, and thus the wages and productivity of truck drivers will decline. Output will be doubly impacted. In the limiting case, when all the returns to trucks are confiscated, no trucks will exist, and the wages accruing to truck drivers will be zero. Output, too, will be zero, as will tax receipts—even though there are no taxes on the earnings of the drivers.

As a pedagogic device, imagine that we reduce the tax rate in the example by one half. The earnings of truck drivers remain untaxed, but now the earnings accruing to trucks are taxed at 50% instead of the previous 100%. Savers who either abstain from consumption or work harder can now obtain an after-tax rate of return by accumulating trucks. There will be more trucks, higher wages, more output, and tax receipts will rise. The increase in tax recipts is an exclusive result of the increase in production and the lowering of tax rates.

A capital gains tax rate cut, armed with the experience of the past decade, addresses the current counter-productive constellation of individual factor tax rates. By partially correcting the stagnatory structures of current tax rates, the bill most likely would lead to a substantial increase in output and, in very short order, a probable reduction in the size of government deficits from what they otherwise would have been. Net revenues could also expand, even though the rate at which capital gains are taxed is reduced. Part of the stated effect on the deficit will occur because higher output means less unemployment, less poverty and therefore lower total spending on unemployment benefits and poverty programs. In this sense, a tax cut would actually reduce government spending and the overall wedge, albeit indirectly.

People do not work and save merely to pay taxes. Businesses do not acquire capital investment as a matter of social conscience. As the Durants pointed out in *Lessons from History*, it is the after-tax incentive that drives production, savings and employment. Other than the taxes levied on the inner-city poor, I know of no factor more discriminated against by our tax structure than is productive capital.

It is not difficult to see the effects of our layering of taxes on capital. Take the example of a machine that earns one dollar of economic profit. Under current required accounting procedures, the actual reported profits for tax purposes will be far higher than one dollar, because of the rules regulating allowable depreciation and inventory valuation adjustments. This machine incurs additional expenses to comply with mandated standards, and for account reporting and other legal services. Most firms feel compelled to monitor various government activities, and these staff costs, too, are partially deducted from the returns to the machine. None of these costs contributes directly to the company's main purpose for existence, its product.

Yet the story has only begun here. The company's capital must also contribute its share to sales, excise, payroll, capital gains and corporate profits taxes. On the same stream of capital, individuals are required to pay personal income taxes ranging in rates up to 70%, as well as personal capital gains taxes. It should be noted that a large part of these capital gains is due purely and simply to rises in the general price level, and thus does not represent an increase in real values.

The effects of the tax policy changes of the Kennedy era are an excellent example of the type of impact we could expect from tax reductions along the lines of the Hansen-Steiger and Roth-Kemp[1] bills. The Kennedy tax program, instituted over a several year period, included an across-the-board cut in personal income tax rates, reduced the corporate tax rate from 52% to 48%, shortened depreciable lives for legal purposes and instituted the investment tax credit. In addition, major tax rate reductions were carried out under the Kennedy tariff cuts.

The numbers look like this. From 1961 to 1966, real GNP grew on average at a 5.4% annual rate. Unemployment rates fell from 6.7% in 1961 to 3.8% in 1966. Capacity utilization (as measured by the Federal Reserve Board) rose from 77.3% in 1961, to 91.1% in 1966. Annual inflation averaged 2.1%, 1.6% and 1.1% for the GNP price deflator, consumer price index and wholesale price index, respectively. If stock prices are any indicator of growth, the ratio of the S&P 500 to GNP went from .110 in 1960 to .115 in 1967. The low was the 1960 ratio, but the peak occurred in 1965 when the ratio hit .128.

During the 1961–66 period, Federal spending rose at a rate lower than GNP growth: 6.2% versus 7.5%. As a consequence, the overall Federal wedge (spending as a percent of GNP) fell from 18.75% in 1961 to 17.62% in 1966. There was a $3.1 billion Federal deficit in 1961, a surplus of $1.4 billion in 1965, and a literal balance in 1966. Defense spending increases during this era were less than non-defense increases. Obviously, the dire consequences predicted for these shocking tax rate cuts did not materialize.

In many ways, we are being visited today by a situation similar to that of 1960. Unemployment is high—currently sitting near 6%. Federal spending, or the aggregate wedge, stands at about 22.6%; S&P stock prices relative to GNP are about .045. The Federal deficit in the most recent period is about $45 billion. Inflation, though, is the real kicker today, hitting well over 6% at annual rates.

In addition to the beneficial effects already mentioned, a tax rate cut on capital gains would have a positive impact on inflation. Inflation is primarily a consequence of too much money chasing too few goods. Excessive money growth has long been recognized as a cause of inflation. It is equally true, however, that too few goods will also cause prices to rise.

To put the relationship into clear focus, imagine the following: What would happen to prices in the United Sates if output were reduced to, say, the output level of Luxembourg, and the amount of money stayed unchanged? Prices would skyrocket, as would unemployment. Higher unemployment means lower output. As such high unemployment is, by itself, a cause of high prices.

In debating a cut in the capital gains tax rate, it is important to recognize that such a cut would be a beginning to meaningful tax reform—not an end. As such, it would not cure our economic ills by itself. Additional legislation such as the Roth-Kemp and Stockman[2] bills would be complementary. Looking into the future, legislation proposing indexing and full integration of the corporate tax

[1] The Roth-Kemp bill would reduce personal tax rates by approximately one-third, and reduce corporate tax rates by three percent over a three-year time period.

[2] Representative Stockman's (R., Michigan) bill, the "Tax Consistency Act," would require replacement cost depreciation allowances for corporations, eliminate the investment tax credit and Domestic International Sales Corporations (DISCs), and reduce the corporate tax rate to 40% from 48%. It would also eliminate excess depletion, bad debt reserves and the shipping industry's capital funds allowance.

structure with personal income taxes is highly desirable. A more distant goal would be a proposal for the substitution of a value-added tax for other, less efficient taxes. Social Security tax and benefit reforms are also badly needed.

It is obvious that our economy is now in trouble; that new solutions are in order. The view that high marginal tax rates can suppress economic activity, and that a rollback of such rates can expand output and, ultimately, tax revenues has two very attractive characteristics. First, and foremost, it is supported by a large body of experience. Second, the policy implications offer some hope to a world afflicted with economic malaise.

In the complex arena of tax legislation, ideal solutions are never arrived at easily, if at all. The capital gains tax rate reductions may not be ideal, but they would provide some immediate relief from the heavy burden of taxation on capital formation. Passage of such a tax cut would be an important step toward further tax reform and a healthier economy.

Statement Before the Subcommittee on Taxation and Debt Management

W. MICHAEL BLUMENTHAL

In the following excerpt from Treasury Secretary W. Michael Blumenthal's testimony on the Steiger-Hansen bill before the Senate Finance Committee's Subcommittee on Taxation and Debt Management, he disputes the bill's claimed ability to achieve middle class tax relief, higher stock prices, increased revenues to the Treasury, and expanded capital formation.

I will devote the bulk of my testimony to S. 3065 [the Steiger-Hansen bill], the "Investment Incentive Act of 1978." To say that this Bill and its House counterpart have received extensive publicity is to engage in understatement. Suddenly, like flowers that bloom in the spring, the notion of reducing capital gains taxation is appearing everywhere as an all-purpose solution to the country's economic problems. Manifold and sweeping claims are made for this idea: It is advertised as a technique of middle class tax relief, or a measure to help homeowners. It is said that reducing capital gains taxes will substantially increase stock values. It is claimed that the Treasury will gain revenues by cutting these taxes. We are told that this is the best way to accelerate capital accumulation in the United States. Some even claim that other economies outperform us because they avoid taxing of capital gains.

This Administration shares the goals espoused by the supporters of a capital gains tax reduction. We too wish to see stock prices rise. We too are concerned about Treasury revenues; and we are certainly as concerned as anyone about reducing the federal deficit. We too are vitally interested in spurring capital accumulation and investment, and believe that tax incentives are needed for this. We too are anxious to employ every reasonable device to improve our performance with respect to inflation, unemployment, and exports.

Our opposition to S. 3065, therefore, is based not on disagreement with its goals. Rather we are persuaded that this bill would not advance us toward these goals or would do so only in ways that are inefficient, inadequate and unjust.

The tax reduction legislation that the Administration has proposed this year would meet two broad objectives:

> First, relief for the average taxpayers of this country who are finding their incomes increasingly pinched by rising tax liabilities.

> Second, a broad and significant increase in the after-tax return on capital, which will increase business investments by making them more attractive.

W. Michael Blumenthal, "Statement on Capital Gains Tax Bills Before the Subcommittee on Taxation and Debt Management of Committee on Finance," June 28, 1978.

Mr. Chairman, a dispassionate and objective analysis of S. 3065 shows that this bill and others like it would achieve neither of these goals while wasting Treasury revenues urgently needed to achieve these critical objectives in an efficient and equitable fashion.

THE FACTS ABOUT CAPITAL GAINS TAXATION UNDER CURRENT LAW

Under current law, the net capital gain of an individual taxpayer is taxed at a rate equal to one-half of the taxpayer's rate on ordinary forms of income, such as wages, salary, dividends, interest, and rent. Those persons in tax brackets above 50% need pay only the 25% alternative rate on the first $50,000 of their net capital gains.

For corporations, net capital gains may be taxed at an "alternative" 30 percent rate instead of the maximum 48 percent rate on other income.

In addition to these basic provisions, the Tax Reform Acts of 1969 and 1976 introduced two elaborations.

First, the 1969 Act imposed a "minimum tax" on those with very large amounts of capital gains income or other income benefitting from preferential provisions. After changes in the 1976 Act, the minimum tax for individuals is 15 percent of preference income in excess of either $10,000 or one-half of regular tax liability (whichever is greater). One-half of capital gain is considered "preference income." Therefore, if a taxpayer's only preference item is capital gain, the minimum tax applies only if total gains exceed $20,000.

Second, the 1969 Act reduced the maximum tax rate on earned income— wages and salaries—from 70 percent to 50 percent, providing massive relief to high-income individuals. For these persons, the amount of earned income eligible for this special "maximum tax" ceiling is offset by the amount of preference income, including the untaxed half of capital gains.

Now, what are the consequences of this structure of capital gains taxation? Who pays what?

In 1978, capital gains taxes will raise $10.3 billion in revenue, $7.8 billion from individuals and $2.5 billion from corporations.

Let's look at the individual side of the equation, where public attention has been concentrated.

The average effective tax rate on capital gains in 1976 was 15.9 percent.... For most Americans with capital gains, the effective rate is quite low: for instance, 12.7 percent for those between $20,000 and $30,000 in adjusted gross income, 16.7 percent for those between $30,000 and $50,000. Up to $200,000 a year, the effective rate is below 25 percent. Even for those over $200,000 the average effective rate is only 27.4 percent.

Typically, therefore, the great majority of taxpayers pays taxes on capital gains at modest levels, considerably below the rate on ordinary earned or unearned income, and the progressiveness of the capital gains tax is quite moderate. The rate generally rises above 25 percent only where the taxpayer's income or gains are extraordinarily large, and even in these instances, the taxes are not at all extreme.

In the current debate, much has been made of the possibility—under the maximum and minimum tax provisions enacted in 1969 and 1976—that individuals may be paying a 50 percent tax or even more on their capital gains. The facts are much less alarming than the rhetoric. Capital gain, at all income levels, is still very much a preference item in our tax system.

More than 60 percent of all capital gains is taxed at 25 percent or less. Of all returns showing capital gains, only about 7 percent is taxed above 25 percent. Though in theory the tax rate could exceed 50 percent, this would require a very implausible composition of income, and in fact we have been unable to find even one case where this has happened. We have found fewer than 20 returns— out of 5.4 million returns with capital gains—taxed at more than 45 percent. The capital gains tax very rarely goes above 40 percent. Rates over 40 percent have appeared in less than five hundredths of one percent of returns with capital gains, involving less than four tenths of one percent of gains.

In sum, the Tax Reform Acts of 1969 and 1976 increased capital gains taxes for very high income individuals with very large gains, but these measures did not introduce unreasonable marginal rates and they left capital gains in a clearly preferred status.

THE FACTS ABOUT S. 3065

This bill is not a general measure to reduce capital gains taxes for everyone. Rather, it aims to reduce the capital gains rate for the highest income individuals with the largest amount of gains. As I have just noted, the overwhelming majority of taxpayers, realizing the great bulk of capital gains each year, pays substantially less than 25 percent on capital gains. This bill is not designed for this vast majority. Its relief is focused almost entirely on the small minority who now pays more than 25 percent.

The bill would do the following. It would remove all non-taxed capital gains income from the minimum tax, rather than exempting the first $10,000 of untaxed gain (or one-half of regular tax liability), as under present law. It would eliminate the present capital gains offset against wage and salary income eligible for the maximum tax. It would extend the 25 percent alternative tax to an unlimited amount of gain, as opposed to the $50,000 of gain eligible for this rate under present law. Finally, it would reduce the "alternative" rate on capital gains for corporations from 30 to 25 percent.

For these changes in the law, very expansive claims have been made. We have examined those claims closely. Few of them stand up against such analysis. At best, it can be said that some of the claims can be neither proven nor disproven. For the most part, however, the claims run flat against the available evidence.

The proponents say that S. 3065 constitutes broad based tax reduction, in line with the so-called "middle class tax revolt." The facts are otherwise. About 20 percent of the bill's benefits would go to corporations. For individuals, the bill's benefits are skewed heavily to the highest income taxpayers. Four-fifths of the bill's benefits go to those with incomes over $100,000 a year. Mr. Chairman, this bill would provide lower taxes for less than one-half of one percent of the individual taxpayers in this country and would benefit only about 7 percent of the taxpayers that have capital gains.

This is in truth a millionaire's relief bill, and I mean *income* millionaires, whose assets are usually many times greater than that. Of those million dollar earners benefitted by S. 3065, about 3,000 of them throughout the country, each would receive on average $214,000 in tax reduction. For all million dollar earners the average relief would be $145,000. By contrast, the average relief for those in the $20,000 to $30,000 class would be one dollar. . . .

The bill's proponents assert that it would trigger a stock market boom. The studies said to show this result simply assume the fact, or rather they assume different facts. Bear in mind that the bill would reduce taxes on corporate stock gains by only $500 million. Yet, one study assumes the bill would raise stock values by 40 percent, a rise of more than $300 billion or 600 times the size of the tax cut; another study suggests only a 4 to 6 percent rise in stock values, which is still 60 times the size of the cut. A third study, which presumes *total* elimination of the capital gains tax, rather than the selective cuts in S. 3065, predicts a 20 percent rise in stock values. This is all the sheerest conjecture. The truth is that no one has any credible evidence or theory permitting a projection of the bill's impact on the stock market, and certainly there is no basis for the extreme assumptions that have dominated public discussion of the bill.

If we look at recent stock market behavior, it is difficult to avoid the conclusion that the effects of capital gains tax changes, if any, are wholly swamped by other stock market influences. The bill's proponents often suggest that the 1969 Tax Reform Act lies behind the stock market's doldrums during the 1970's. However, the stock market fell sharply in 1969, before the tax increases from the Reform Act took effect. Then the market rebounded sharply from 1970 through 1972—the same period during which the reforms were fully phased in. Then, as inflationary momentum accelerated in 1973, there was a huge fall in stock prices, though the tax law was not changed at all. . . .

Analysis of stock market prices over the last ten years shows no relationship between the capital gains tax and the market's level. The record does not show that the capital gains tax changes in the Reform Acts of 1969 and 1976 depressed stock prices. The assertion that repeal of those reforms would now raise stock prices is just that, an assertion, unsupported by evidence.

Proponents of S. 3065 have noted that it would provide relief for homeowners forced to pay capital gains taxes upon sale of their residences, in those instances where the gain cannot be rolled over into purchase of a new residence. This aspect of the measure, we wholeheartedly support. The President's tax package provides nearly identical relief for homeowners.

A further claim of the proponents is that this bill would greatly spur capital formation. Accelerating the rate of capital formation—particularly industrial and technological investment—is a priority objective of this Administration, but S. 3065 is not the way to go about it.

Why is this so? The test of a tax cut for investment is how generally and directly it reduces the tax burden on income from productive capital. In applying this test, it is important to keep in mind two facts. First, productive capital is taxed in many ways—by the corporate income tax, the individual income tax, the capital gains tax, etc. We don't have a single, unique tax on capital income; rather we have many taxes which together place a burden on capital. Capital gains tax is *not* the major tax on capital income. It accounts for only about 10 percent of the federal tax burden on capital. . . .

Second, the kind of capital we particularly need to accumulate is industrial and technological capital. Many types of assets—for instance jewelry, antiques, speculative real estate, and the like—are of much less importance to our economy's ability to adapt, grow, and compete in international markets. The President's tax proposal takes these two important facts into account. Through broad based reductions in corporate and individual income tax rates, and through a liberalization of the investment tax credit, the President's package would reduce the major taxes burdening capital income by about $7 billion and would directly increase the profitability and cash flow of all productive enterprises. It is a package ideally suited to increasing the rate of formation of productive capital.

By contrast, S. 3065 is very poorly suited to this job. As I've noted, capital gains taxes constitute only about 10 percent of the federal tax burden on capital income. Reducing the capital gains tax would therefore deal with only a very small corner of the problem. Furthermore, it is in many respects the wrong corner. Only about one-quarter of realized capital gains come from corporate stock. The rest are scattered over a range of assets having little or no role to play in the kind of investment boom this country needs. For instance, another quarter of the realizations is on real estate sales, 3.4 percent on livestock, 2.5 percent on commodities, 9.7 percent on installment sales, etc. . . . This bill would create windfalls on assets all over the landscape, but it would largely detour around the central objective, which is to reduce significantly and broadly the tax burden on income from productive investment. This bill takes a very inefficient approach to capital formation.

This inefficiency is a fatal flaw for the simple reason that we do not have unlimited revenues available to stimulate capital formation. To keep the budget deficit in bounds, the Administration believes next year's total tax reduction should not exceed $20 billion. The bill before you would take up over $2 billion of that amount. This would have to come at the expense of wage and salary earners, which would be clearly inequitable, or at the expense of the corporate income tax reductions, which would render the bill a much less effective vehicle for capital formation. The only other choice is to increase the budget deficit, which would be an inflationary and irresponsible course.

The proponents of S. 3065 try to avoid this dilemma by asserting that their bill, unlike the myriad other tax cuts promoted in the Congress, would in fact increase Treasury revenues.

The reasoning behind this assertion has never been made clear. As is often the case with this subject, we are dealing here with conjecture, not facts.

It is important, in assessing the revenue claims, to distinguish between three different time horizons: the very short term, the medium term, and the long term.

In the short term, the revenue impact of S. 3065 would turn on the so-called "unlocking" effect. With a cut in maximum capital gains rates, it is possible, at least in theory, that some taxpayers would sell assets that they had held for a very long time. Whether and how much this would occur, no one knows. If it did happen, two results would follow. First, the wave of selling might well depress asset prices, on the stock market and elsewhere. This would tend to reduce capital gains tax revenues. Second, the wave of selling would itself generate tax revenues. The net effect on revenues of these conflicting forces, no one can predict. But one thing is clear: It would be a temporary, one-shot effect. The wave of selling would not repeat itself year after year.

In the medium term, *any* tax reduction will stimulate aggregate demand—

investment and consumption—and therefore tend to increase GNP toward its potential level, creating a "feedback" of tax revenues to the Treasury. There is absolutely no reason to think that S. 3065 would create larger feedback effects than any other cut in capital income taxes. Indeed, such feedback effects are much less certain with capital gains taxes than with the corporate income tax cuts proposed by the President. Cutting corporate rates and liberalizing the investment tax credit would directly increase enterprise profits and cash flow, and thus real investment and tax revenues. The advocates of S. 3065 hold out the hope—no more—that a capital gains tax cut would substantially boost stock values and that this in turn would trigger a large amount of new investment, with a consequent rise in tax revenues. But, as I have indicated, there is no perceptible relationship between capital gains taxes and the level of the stock market, and a capital gains tax cut of this size is most unlikely to affect the stock market substantially. Unfortunately, it is equally difficult to trace a causal relationship between the level of the stock market and the rate of increase of investment or GNP. Both points in the argument are thus very shaky. For the medium term, the revenue feedback effect of a capital gains tax reduction is anyone's guess.

In the long term—the most important perspective—tax revenues depend on the sustained growth rate of the economy. In other words, the revenue feedback will be greater the more efficiently the tax cut boosts the long term trend of investment in productive assets and enterprises. It is precisely here that S. 3065 is most seriously defective. It scatters its benefits over a wide array of assets, many of little productivity, and it misses entirely 90 percent of the tax burden on capital income. It is a very poor tool for increasing the economy's long term rate of real growth, and its long term revenue feedback effects would be commensurately modest.

Finally, I wish to say a word about the very loose international comparisons that have been made in the debate on this measure. Some proponents of S. 3065 have suggested that our economic performance—in areas of inflation, unemployment, and growth—has fallen short of that of Germany and Japan because we tax capital gains while they, assertedly, do not. This line of argument ignores certain important facts. First, the United States has over the past few years outperformed most other industrialized countries, including Germany and Japan, in terms of real growth and increases in employment. Our inflation record is less satisfactory, but is nonetheless superior to several countries (e.g. Italy) having no capital gains tax. Second, Japan does in fact tax capital gains. As for Germany, it instead uses an even more comprehensive tax on annual increases in wealth, whether or not realized; I doubt that the proponents of S. 3065 would prefer the German system to ours. What all this shows is that making simplistic international comparisons on a tax-by-tax basis is a very treacherous business.

In sum, Mr. Chairman, the claims made for S. 3065 do not stand up to scrutiny:

- The bill would not provide general or middle income tax relief but would instead narrowly focus its benefits on the highest income classes and would provide an unprecedented boon to millionaires.

- The bill has no realistic potential for creating a substantial rise in stock prices.

- The bill would not efficiently meet our urgent needs for more investment in productive enterprises.

- The bill would not gain us revenue but would instead use up revenue needed for far more efficient and equitable incentives for capital formation.

There are of course many variations of S. 3065 under discussion in the other Chamber. I will not deal with them in detail. Some of the proposals escape certain problems I have noted here. However, those involving an effective repeal of the minimum tax so far as capital gains are concerned have the same defects as S. 3065: they are very expensive, and they focus their benefits on a narrow class of extremely high income individuals, with the result that many of those persons would pay very little tax. As the President has indicated, this is an unfair and ineffective response to the need of American workers and businesses for genuine tax reduction. . . .

CONCLUSION

The various federal taxes on capital income—the capital gains provisions, the corporate income tax, and the personal income tax on property income—make up an interrelated and complicated structure. The Treasury is now engaged in a far-reaching study of that structure, seeking to determine how it might best be rationalized in light of the capital formation problems our economy faces, and will continue to face, over the coming years. I am giving this study my closest personal attention. None of us is bringing rigid views on the taxation of capital gains into this exercise. But tinkering with bits and pieces of this structure of capital income taxation—as the bills before you do—will get us nowhere. The whole structure will become that much more complex, inequitable, inefficient, and incoherent. In the process, we will lose revenues critically needed for more efficient investment incentives. To deal properly with the capital gains tax, what is required is a thoughtful and comprehensive approach to capital income taxation generally.

Inflation and Capital Formation

MARTIN FELDSTEIN

In recent years, inflation has pushed the effective tax rate on investment income into the prohibitively high range. In the following editorial from *The Wall Street Journal*, Martin Feldstein, president of the National Bureau of Economic Research and professor of economics at Harvard University, specifies how our tax system has been impaired by inflation. He devotes special attention to the importance of replacing the current method of calculating depreciation to protect it from the hazards of inflation.

During the past decade, effective tax rates have increased dramatically on capital gains, on interest income and on the direct returns to investment in plant and equipment. Investors in stocks and bonds now pay tax rates of nearly 100%—and in many cases more than 100%—on their real returns.

This change has taken place without public debate and without legislative action, though Tuesday's vote by the House Ways and Means Committee to "index" capital gains may finally have placed the matter on the political agenda. Our tax system was designed for an economy with little or no inflation. But if current rates of inflation persist, the existing tax laws will continue to impose effective tax rates of more than 100% on investment incomes. To make matters even worse, the current tax laws imply that future tax rates will depend haphazardly on future rates of inflation and therefore cannot be predicted at the time that investment decisions are being made.

These extremely high tax rates and the uncertainty about future tax rates are a cloud that hangs over both the stock market and business investment decisions. Several recent studies at the National Bureau of Economic Research [NBER] that quantify the effect of inflation on the taxation of investment income and therefore on the incentive to investment show these dramatic effects.

A SUBSTANTIAL INCREASE

Inflation is particularly harsh on the taxation of capital gains. Under current law, when corporate stock or any other asset is sold, a capital gains tax must be paid on the entire difference between the selling price and the original cost even though much of the nominal gain only offsets a general rise in the prices of consumer goods and services. Taxing *nominal* gains in this way very substantially increases the effective tax rate on *real* price-adjusted gains. Indeed, many individuals pay a substantial capital gains tax even though, when adjustment is made for the change in the price level, they actually receive less from their sale than they had originally paid.

In a recent study at the National Bureau of Economic Research, Joel Slemrod and I measured the total excess taxation of corporate stock capital gains caused by inflation and the extent to which this distortion differs capriciously

Martin Feldstein, "Inflation and Capital Formation," *The Wall Street Journal*, July 27, 1978, p. 12. Reprinted by permission of *The Wall Street Journal*, ©Dow Jones & Company, Inc., 1978. All Rights Reserved.

among individuals. We found that in 1973 individuals paid capital gains tax on $4.6 billion of nominal capital gains on corporate stock. When the costs of these shares are adjusted for the increase in the consumer price level since they were purchased, this gain becomes a loss of nearly $1 billion.

The $4.6 billion of nominal capital gains resulted in a tax liability of $1.1 billion. The tax liability on the real capital gains would have been only $661 million. Inflation thus raised tax liabilities by nearly $500 million, approximately doubling the overall effective tax rate on corporate stock capital gains.

Although adjusting for the price change reduces the gain at every income level, the effect of the price level correction is far from uniform. In particular, the mismeasurement of capital gains is most severe for taxpayers with incomes under $100,000.

In the highest income class, there is little difference between nominal and real capital gains; in contrast, taxpayers with incomes below $100,000 suffered real capital losses even though they were taxed on positive nominal gains. In each income class up to $50,000, recognizing real capital gains makes the tax liability negative. At higher income levels, tax liabilities are reduced but remain positive on average; the extent of the current excess tax decreases with income.

Inflation not only raises the effective tax rate, but also makes the taxation of capital gains arbitrary and capricious. Individuals who face the same statutory rates have their real capital gains taxed at very different rates because of differences in holding periods. For example, among taxpayers with adjusted gross incomes of $20,000 to $50,000, we found that only half of the tax liability on capital gains was incurred by taxpayers whose liabilities on real gains would have been between 80% and 100% of their actual liabilities. The remaining half of tax liabilities were incurred by individuals whose liabilities on real gains would have been less than 80% of their actual statutory liabilities.

In short, our study showed that inflation has substantially increased— roughly doubled—the overall effective tax rate on corporate stock capital gains. Although this estimate relates to 1973 (because that is the only year for which data of this type are available), the continuing high rate of inflation means that the tax distortion for more recent years is likely to be even greater.

The second major problem that inflation causes in our tax system is in the treatment of depreciation. Under current law, the amount of depreciation that is allowed on any asset depends on its original cost. When inflation raises the price level, the real value of these depreciation allowances is reduced. This reduction in the real value of depreciation that is caused by the historic cost method of depreciation is equivalent to a substantial increase in the rate of tax on corporate and other investment income.

In 1977, the historic cost method of tax depreciation caused corporate depreciation to be understated by more than $30 billion. This understatement increased corporate tax liabilities by $15 billion, a 25% increase in corporate taxes. This extra inflation tax reduced net profits by 28% of the total 1977 net profits of $53 billion. This is the single most important adverse effect of inflation on capital formation.

This brings me to the final tax problem caused by inflation, the failure to distinguish between nominal interest and real interest. This problem is fundamentally different from the problems involved in capital gains taxation and in depreciation. The nature of this difference is still not widely appreciated. The difference is extremely important, however, because it implies that changing the tax treatment of interest is less urgent than the other changes. Let me explain why.

It is clear that taxing *nominal* interest income imposes an unfair burden on bond owners and other lenders. But allowing a deduction for nominal interest expenses also provides an unfair benefit to corporations and other borrowers. When markets have had a chance to respond fully to the higher rate of inflation, interest rates will adjust to reduce the unfair burden on lenders and to reduce the unfair advantage of borrowers.

If all borrowers and lenders had the same marginal tax rate, the market adjustment of interest rates could eliminate all inequities, leaving borrowers and lenders with the same real after-tax rates of interest that they would face in the absence of inflation.

Let me emphasize, however, that this rough, long-run justice would only be achieved if the current method of depreciation is replaced by price-indexed or current cost depreciation. If we stay with our current system of depreciation, interest rates will fail to adjust fully and bondholders will suffer a substantial permanent fall in their real after-tax returns.

In a recent NBER study Lawrence Summers and I showed that, roughly speaking, with our current system of depreciation and taxation, each 1% rise in the expected rate of inflation will induce a 1% rise in the market rate of interest. The real rate of interest will remain unchanged, but the real *after-tax* rate of interest will fall sharply. This is, in effect, the mechanism by which firms transfer some of the adverse effect of historic cost depreciation to bondholders.

The magnitude of this effect is large enough to imply effective tax rates of more than 100% on interest income. Consider what has happened since the early 1960s. The inflation rate was then only 1%, and the 5% nominal yield on Baa bonds provided a real yield of 4%. An investor with a 40% marginal rate obtained an after-tax yield of 3%, and a *real* after-tax yield of 2%. By comparison, during the past three years a Baa bond yielded 10%, but consumer prices rose 6%. An investor with a 40% marginal rate obtained a 6% after-tax yield but a *real* after-tax yield of zero. In short, the effective rate of tax on real income was 100%.

IMPERFECT, BUT . . .

The meaning of this calculation is clear. If historic cost depreciation is continued, taxpaying bondholders will receive little or no after-tax income. This can be remedied by allowing bondholders and other lenders to include only *real* interest receipts in their taxable income. But this should be seen as only an imperfect way of dealing with the more basic problem of depreciation. Moreover, it is important to limit this change in the treatment of interest to bond holders; reducing the deduction taken by corporations to their real interest payments without adjusting depreciation rules would only transfer the full burden of mismeasuring depreciation to equity investors.

Replacing the current method of depreciation is, therefore, the key problem. If this is done, adjusting the taxation of interest income is of secondary importance. The specific method of depreciation that is adopted—replacement cost depreciation, general price indexing or immediate expensing of investment—is a much less important issue than the general principle that the value of depreciation must be insulated from the effects of inflation.

5/
PROPOSITION 13—
THE JARVIS-GANN INITIATIVE

Following a period of spectacular increases in property values in California—many homes doubled and tripled in value during the 1970s—the voters in that state demanded a halt to the drastic increase in associated property taxes. Approved by an astonishing two-thirds margin, Proposition 13, the Jarvis-Gann initiative, became the weapon with which voters struck down high property taxes and put Sacramento, and government officials in general, on notice that they had better be responsive to the electorate.

Beginning with fiscal year 1978–1979, Proposition 13 limits to 1 percent of full cash value the amount of property taxes that can be collected from an owner of county-assessed real property. This limit could be exceeded only to raise revenue to pay bonded debt approved by the voters before July 1, 1978. "Full cash value" is defined as the county assessor's valuation of the real property as shown on the 1975–1976 tax bill. The assessment freeze will allow for an inflationary increase of no more than 2 percent a year unless the property is sold or transferred or new construction has occurred. In the latter cases, the assessment would be raised to reflect the market value resulting from each of these events.

Proposition 13 requires a two-thirds vote in each house of the legislature to increase state taxes, and it prohibits the legislature from enacting any new taxes based on the value or sale of real property.

Cities, counties, and special districts may impose special taxes on approval of two-thirds of the qualified electors provided the taxes are not based on the value or sale of real property.

Supporters of the initiative believe that the limited property tax revenues will still cover property-related government services, will make rent reductions probable, will bring new business into California, and will create new jobs. Arguments against Proposition 13 focus on the inequitable treatment of property owners caused by the exceptions to the assessment freeze. Opponents fear that the tax cut will require either offsetting increases in taxes and costs elsewhere or severe cutbacks in necessary services.

In the articles that follow we present several diverse opinions on the many issues surrounding the Jarvis-Gann initiative, including its implications for the federal government.

Proposition 13:
Its Impact on the Nation's Economy, Federal Revenues, and Federal Expenditures

CONGRESSIONAL BUDGET OFFICE

In view of the considerable margin by which Proposition 13 was passed in California, and of the fact that other states will most likely follow suit and enter into the tax revolt, the Congressional Budget Office prepared an analysis of the possible effects Proposition 13 may have on the national economy. Included here are the introduction and summary of the analysis, which provide some insight into the interrelationship between changes in state property taxes and changes in the Consumer Price Index, federal income taxes, and federal spending programs.

Proposition 13, an amendment to the California Constitution that limits local property tax rates and makes it more difficult to increase other state and local taxes, will reduce the property tax revenues of California local governments by some $7,044 million in fiscal year 1978–1979.[1] Spending cutbacks will not be as deep as implied by the revenue loss because the state has agreed to distribute $4,122 million of its accumulated surplus to its local governments; because some localities have surpluses of their own to tap; and because some jurisdictions will raise fees, users' charges, and nonproperty taxes.

In the near term, Proposition 13 will have an insignificant effect on the nation's economy. The property tax cut will stimulate economic activity, but only slowly because much of it will be retained by businesses. It will also lead to a lower price level because property taxes are a part of the housing component of the Consumer Price Index (CPI). The cutbacks in state and local spending resulting from Proposition 13, however, should depress the economy. On balance Proposition 13 will cause:

- Marginally lower levels of real economic activity through the first half of calendar year 1979 and marginally higher levels of real activity by mid-1980.

- An employment loss of about 60,000 by the end of 1978 that will gradually diminish in size.

[1]The fiscal year in California runs from July 1 to June 30 and is indicated in this paper by "fiscal year" followed by two hyphenated years. "Fiscal year" followed by a single year refers to the federal fiscal year, which runs from October 1 to September 30.

Proposition 13: Its Impact on the Nation's Economy, Federal Revenues, and Federal Expenditures, Washington, D.C.: Congress of the United States, Congressional Budget Office, July 1978, pp. ix–x, 1–4.

- A reduction in the Consumer Price Index of 0.2 percent by the end of 1978 and 0.4 percent by mid-1980.

Federal revenues should increase by about $600 million in fiscal year 1979 and $900 million in fiscal year 1980 because of Proposition 13. These increases are the net result of two offsetting factors. First, because individual and business taxpayers will have smaller property tax deductions to claim on their federal tax returns, federal corporate and individual income tax collections will rise. Second, the impact of Proposition 13 on the price level and on the level of economic activity will lower the current dollar value of national income and this, taken alone, will cause federal tax collections to be lower than they would have been in the absence of Proposition 13.

Total federal expenditures will not be significantly affected by Proposition 13. Expenditure cutbacks by California and its localities will lead to layoffs that could increase spending for transfer programs such as unemployment compensation and food stamps. On the other hand, the impact of the property tax cut on the price level will lower anticipated federal spending for social security, civil service retirement, and other programs whose spending levels are tied directly or indirectly to the CPI.

Expenditure cutbacks could lead to lower federal spending by reducing California's participation in federal grant programs that have matching requirements. For example, an expected denial of the cost-of-living increase in welfare benefits will simultaneously reduce federal as well as state and local expenditures. Budget cuts could also lead to California governments violating the maintenance of effort provisions contained in many federal grant programs. The employment and training, education, and transit areas appear to be the most susceptible to this situation occurring. Overall, however, these provisions are not expected to pose serious problems. Moreover, while California may lose some federal aid, much of this money would be reallocated to other states at a later date. Thus, while the level of federal spending in the near term might be lower than would be the case if Proposition 13 had not been adopted, it could be higher after the funds are reallocated.

Many of the factors thought to be responsible for the passage of Proposition 13—the high tax rates, rapid rate of tax increases, and presence of surpluses—are not conditions unique to California. Thus similar taxpayer revolts could occur elsewhere or public officials could attempt to preempt such revolts by providing tax relief before required to do so by the voters. Such relief is likely to be financed by slowing the rate of increase in expenditures and by spending down surpluses rather than by cutting back real service levels. If such actions spread to a significant number of states, the impact on the nation's economy and the federal budget could become significant. Unless the reductions in taxes are at least twice as large as the accompanying slowdown or cut in expenditures, the net effect is likely to be a slowdown in economic activity and employment growth. . . .

DESCRIPTION OF PROPOSITION 13

Proposition 13 places restrictions on property tax rates, assessment practices, and increases in state taxes and local special taxes. Specifically:

- Property tax rates will be limited to 1 percent of full cash value plus the rate needed to service bonded indebtedness approved by the voters before the beginning of fiscal year 1978–1979. The one percent rate will be levied by each county and divided in proportion to past property tax collections among the county government and the municipalities, school districts, and special districts within the county.[2]

- Assessed values—which are supposed to be 25 percent of full value—will be rolled back to the levels on the 1975–1976 assessment rolls; where these levels do not reflect a property's 1975 value, the assessment will be increased to this level. Assessed values will be increased annually to reflect inflation, but by no more than 2 percent per year. Upon sale a property will be reassessed at its market value if that value exceeds the 1975–1976 assessment adjusted by 2 percent per year. Newly constructed properties will be assessed at market value.

- Statutes to increase state taxes will have to be approved by two-thirds of the elected members of each of the Legislature's two houses and no new state ad-valorem, sales, or transaction tax on real property will be permitted.

- Special taxes, except for taxes on real property, can be imposed by local governments only after approval by two-thirds of the jurisdiction's voters and only if such taxes conform to the powers granted to the locality under the state's statutes and constitution. The two-thirds restriction presumably would not apply to taxes proposed for general purposes (for example, local sales tax) by a general local government (that is, a city or county).

Initially, Proposition 13 will reduce the total revenues of local governments by 23 percent. School districts, which rely heavily on property taxes, would be most affected; cities and nonenterprise special districts, the least (see Table 1 [on page 113]).[3]

Of the $7,044 million reduction in property tax payments, about one-third will accrue initially to homeowners and 17 percent to owners of rental units (see Table 2). Commercial, industrial, and agricultural property owners will receive 41 percent of the reduction. The remainder will represent savings to the state government in the form of reduced state tax relief subventions that replace local revenues lost because of homeowner and business inventory exemptions.

---

[2]The rate required to service voter-approved bonded indebtedness is estimated to average about 0.25 percent. Under a recently enacted law, the pro-rata distribution of the receipts from the county-wide one percent tax will be allocated in proportion to the three-year average of tax collections by the county government, each municipality and special district, and the tax collections for fiscal year 1978-1979 for each school district.

[3]Enterprise special districts run such activities as electric and water utilities, waste disposal, transit, hospitals, and airports. Nonenterprise special districts provide such services as fire protection, flood control, local and regional planning, recreation, parks, and streets and roads.

TABLE 1

Revenue Loss Resulting from Proposition 13, by Type of Government, Fiscal Year 1978–1979

	Revenue Loss (in millions of dollars)	AS A PERCENT OF:	
		Property Tax Receipts	Total Revenues
Cities a	806	60.0	15.2
Counties b	2,236	58.8	28.9
School Districts	3,539	54.7	29.2
Special Districts (Enterprise)	216	55.7	22.4
Special Districts (Nonenterprise)	247	55.8	5.6
Total	7,044	56.6	23.4

Source: Summary of the California Legislature Conference Report on SB 154 Relative to Implementation of Proposition 13 and State Assistance to Local Governments, June 23, 1978.
a Excludes San Francisco.
b Includes San Francisco.

TABLE 2

Distribution of Initial Tax Relief, by Type of Property, Fiscal Year 1978–1979

	Initial Tax Relief (millions of dollars)	As a Percent of Total Relief
Owner-Occupied Residential	2,341	33.2
Rental-Occupied Residential	1,200	17.0
Commercial and Industrial	1,916	27.2
Agricultural	944	13.4
State	643	9.1
Total	7,044	100.0

Source: Legislative Analyst, An Analysis of Proposition 13, The Jarvis-Gann Property Tax Initiative, May 1978, California Legislature, Sacramento, California.

Punching Through the Jarvis Myth

WILLIAM SCHNEIDER

William Schneider, associate professor of government at Harvard University, worked at the Hoover Institution during Summer 1978 and was a consultant to the *Los Angeles Times* during the June 6, 1978, primary election. In the following editorial, he explores the reasons behind the massive victory of Proposition 13. Based on a poll taken by the *Los Angeles Times*-Channel 2 News Survey, the two factors that emerge as the major determinants of the vote on June 6th are self-interest and ideology. One of Schneider's most significant interpretations of the election outcome is that it was a vote against high taxes, *not* against government spending.

"The baby got hold of the hammer." That's the way one commentator saw the results of the Proposition 13 vote as the figures came rolling out of the computer on Tuesday night.

On Wednesday, Sen. Alan Cranston remarked that "Jarvis-Gann is like that two-by-four you're supposed to hit a mule with to get its attention." And Patricia Harris, President Carter's Secretary of Housing and Urban Development, said that the vote in California was "rather like burning down a barn to roast a pig when there are some easier ways to do it."

The judgment of most moderate and responsible politicians is that the voters of California behaved in an immoderate and irresponsible manner by turning out in record numbers to pass Proposition 13, the "Jarvis-Gann" Property Tax Initiative, by a window-rattling 65% to 35% majority.

Just what were the voters trying to say?

There is no question that the voters knew exactly what they were doing Proposition 8, the more "moderate and responsible" property-tax relief measure supported by Gov. Brown and the state Legislature, was rejected, 53% to 47% Indeed, *The Los Angeles Times*-Channel 2 News Survey, in which almost 2,500 voters filled out questionnaires as they left the polls Tuesday, revealed that Propositions 8 and 13 were seen by most voters as mutually exclusive alternatives, even though it was entirely possible for voters to play it safe by voting for both measures.

Among those who voted for Proposition 13, only one in five also voted for Proposition 8, while Proposition 8 was endorsed by fully 91% of those who voted "no" on Proposition 13. Proposition 13 was advertised as a stronger tax-relief measure than Proposition 8. That is exactly how the voters saw it, and that is exactly what they wanted.

A careful inspection of the survey results turns up two factors which explain the vote on Proposition 13.

One is self-interest. It was in the interest of most voters to have their prop

William Schneider, "Punching Through the Jarvis Myth," *Los Angeles Times*, June 11, 1978, Part IV, p 1. Reprinted by permission of the author.

erty taxes lowered. We knew this because the survey allowed us to separate out those voters who did not have such an interest. The latter included renters, who do not pay property taxes directly, and public employees, for whom Proposition 13 meant a possible loss of employment.

Voters whose households included public employes and who lived in rental housing voted only 28% in favor of Proposition 13—and 80% in favor of Proposition 8. Voters for whom only one of these conditions applied—either rental housing or public employment—split their votes almost evenly on both measures. And voters who owned their own homes and who had no public employes in their households voted overwhelmingly for Proposition 13—81% "yes," 19% "no"—and rejected Proposition 8 by almost as decisive a margin.

The problem for opponents of Proposition 13 was that two thirds of the voters on June 6 owned their own homes and two thirds had no public employes in the family. Over half of the electorate June 6 fell into the category where these two conditions intersected—homeowners with no public employes in the family. This group, of course, had the highest interest in property-tax relief. Fewer than one voter in 10 fell into the category with the opposite characteristics, that is, the category which had a very low interest in property-tax relief.

The self-interest component of the vote can be seen in the county returns as well. There were three counties which Proposition 13 failed to carry. One was San Francisco, a county dominated by renters. Another was Yolo, a county dominated by state employes. The third was Kern, a wealthy agricultural county in which property taxes have not increased at nearly the rate found in other, more suburban and residential counties.

The second factor that explains the Proposition 13 vote is ideology. The Los Angeles Times-Channel 2 News Survey asked voters to describe their political views as either liberal, moderate or conservative. The vote for Proposition 13 increased from 45% among self-described liberals, to 65% among moderates, to 82% among conservatives. The vote for Proposition 8 increased in the opposite direction. Only 2% of self-described conservatives voted for Proposition 8, but the percentage of "yes" ballots on Proposition 8 rose to 47% among moderates and 63% among liberals. Thus, the effect of ideology was strong and consistent: Proposition 13 was the "conservative alternative," while Proposition 8 appealed disproportionately to liberals.

Still, it is worth emphasizing that 45% of the liberals did vote in favor of Proposition 13, and so did 40% of blacks for that matter. Clearly, self-interest cross-cut ideology and brought many blacks and liberals over to the "yes on 13" side.

When one takes both interest and ideology into account, the vote on Proposition 13 has been largely explained. Voters in the high self-interest category (homeowners with no public employes in the household) gave Proposition 13 a majority of their votes, whether they were liberal, moderate or conservative.

And Proposition 13 carried among all conservatives, even those who rented and worked for the government. The vote among conservatives who owned their homes and did not work for the government was almost unanimous—90% in favor of Proposition 13. The vote among liberals who were renters and public employes was at the opposite extreme—only 19% favorable.

Proposition 13 created a coalition of interest and ideology. Interest was by far the more important factor however. Over half of the voters fell into the high interest category as described above. But only 28% of the voters called themselves conservatives.

The evidence also suggests that these groups had different reasons for supporting Proposition 13. In both The Times-Channel 2 polls and a similar survey taken on election day by NBC News and the Associated Press, two reasons for their stand were most frequently given by supporters of Proposition 13: High property taxes and waste in government. Over half of the respondents who voted for Proposition 13 in The Times-Channel 2 poll explained their vote with the statement "Property taxes should be lowered." Only 22% gave the reason, "Government provides many unnecessary services."

The view that "property taxes should be lowered" tended to be much stronger among homeowners as compared with renters for obvious reasons. But liberals, moderates and conservatives did not differ very much on this point. The difference between liberals, moderates and conservatives was much greater over the issue of whether "government provides many unnecessary services." Conservatives were much more likely than liberals to feel that this was the case.

It appears that the primary concern of the "self-interested" voters, who made up most of the "yes on 13" coalition, was to lower taxes. Conservatives shared this concern, but added to it a strong hostility to government. Conservatives saw Proposition 13 as a way to do what conservatives have been trying to do for almost 50 years—stop the growth of government. The telling point is that when respondents were asked "Do you think local services will be reduced if Proposition 13 passes?" less than a quarter of those who voted for Jarvis-Gann said "yes."

Seventy-one percent of the "yes on 13" voters thought that they could obtain drastic property tax reduction without any significant reductions in government services—unrealistic perhaps, but hardly indicative of a deep antipathy toward government.

Thus, it would be a mistake to interpret the Proposition 13 vote as more than what it was. It was a vote against high taxes. The property tax is a particularly good target because it is billed and not withheld, because its rate of increase in most areas has been truly outrageous, and because it taxes what most Americans regard as an essential component of success and security—owning your own home.

The "yes on 13" forces pointedly advertised their campaign as one to "save the American Dream."

Conservatives oppose high taxes like everyone else, but they also oppose government spending and the expansion of public services in principle. Inflation—the increase in the cost of everything, including the cost of government—has given conservatives a powerful ally in their anti-government crusade: the mass of homeowners, taxpayers and consumers who "are mad as hell and aren't going to take it anymore."

There is no evidence that these voters are opposed to government in principle. They are simply opposed to more government than they can afford. Voters respond to the choices available to them. The choice presented by Proposition 13 was, "Do you want to achieve a massive reduction in property taxes or not?" The answer, not surprisingly, was a defiant "yes." Proposition 13 was the first major ballot issue anywhere in America which asked voters to respond to inflation in clear and direct terms. It may well represent the first in a nationwide wave of anti-inflation protest votes. It is not surprising that the anti-inflation protest is taking the form of a tax revolt: Taxes are the only "prices" that people can vote on. All other price increases, like postal rates, are simply declared, and people are forced to live with them.

Thus, it would be a mistake to read the vote on Proposition 13 as a massive crusade against government or as a conversion of the voters to conservatism. But it would also be a mistake to underestimate this landslide. The voters want—indeed, demand—that some way be found to alleviate the tax burden. Elimination of waste and frills in government is certainly called for. But few voters really want to eliminate the wide variety of government services which they regard as essential. This was not clear from the Proposition 13 vote simply because it was not asked on the ballot. Elimination of government services, The Times-Channel 2 poll showed, was much more on the minds of opponents of Proposition 13 than on those of its supporters.

Thus, the issue raised by Jarvis-Gann is more technical and economic than it is ideological. Gov. Brown would be well advised to come up with a solution—and fast.

The Jarvis-Gann Tax Cut Proposal: An Application of the Laffer Curve

CHARLES W. KADLEC AND ARTHUR B. LAFFER

In the study of the Jarvis-Gann initiative that follows, Charles W. Kadlec and Arthur B. Laffer, both of H. C. Wainwright and Co., found that the proposed 50 percent cut in property tax rates would lead within ten years to an estimated $110 billion increase in California personal income. This expansion of the state's economy could result in more total tax revenues for state and local governments and, combined with the directly implied decrease in unemployment and social welfare spending, would result in an increased budget surplus.

On June 6th, Californians approved Proposition 13—popularly known as the Jarvis-Gann initiative. Property tax rates on homes, businesses and farms will be cut more than 50% to a rate of 1% of a property's 1975–76 assessed market value. Moreover, future tax rate increases will be curtailed sharply. Increases in tax collections from the reassessment of property will be limited to 2% a year as long as the property is not sold. And, the majority required in the state legislature to increase any other tax rate will be increased to two-thirds from a simple majority today.

Without considering any other economic effects, the tax rate cut will reduce property tax revenues from an estimated $12.5 billion in 1978–79 to about $5.5 billion. As a result, many California businessmen, who fear higher non-property business taxes to maintain current spending levels; banks, who are understandably concerned about the values of their municipal bond portfolios; and public employee labor unions, who fear layoffs; all oppose the tax cut. And, Moody's Investors Services, Inc. has suspended its rating on the existing $1.6 billion outstanding tax-allocation bonds from California.

In our view, their concerns are exaggerated for two reasons:

1. Property tax revenues will fall by less than $7 billion because of an increase in the property tax base.

2. Total tax revenues most likely will rise because the increase in general economic activity in California will produce significantly higher income, sales and other tax revenues.

THE ECONOMIC IMPACT

An immediate effect of approval of Proposition 13 will be a decrease in the after-tax cost of home ownership. As a result, demand for single family homes

Charles W. Kadlec and Arthur B. Laffer, *The Jarvis-Gann Tax Cut Proposal: An Application of the Laffer Curve* (Boston: H. C. Wainwright & Co., 1978). Reprinted by permission of H. C. Wainwright & Co.

will increase and the market value of housing will rise. Higher property values, in turn, will spur new housing construction. Thus, in short order, the higher value of homes and the lower after-tax cost of home ownership will increase both the supply and demand for single family homes.

Similarly, the cost of rental housing will fall and the supply of multi-family units will rise. Current rents reflect, in part, the rent-versus-buy cost trade-off to the household, and the alternative uses of capital for rental-unit owners. Thus, the cost reduction of home-ownership implied by passage of Jarvis-Gann will reduce rents until the cost trade-off is restored. Just as important, the property tax rate cut will increase the after-tax rate of return on rental units. Since capital employed in rental housing is a close substitute for capital employed elsewhere, this increase will attract more capital and lead to the construction of more apartment units until the profitability of rental units returns to its market-determined equilibrium level. The increased supply of rental units also will cause rents to fall. Again, both the supply and demand for rental units will rise to a new equilibrium level.

Businesses also will be affected by the property tax cut. The after-tax cost of locating offices or plants in California will fall, thereby increasing demand for California real estate. And, the after-tax returns to owners of commercial property will jump, leading to increased construction of commercial and industrial facilities.

Combined, the expected increases in supply and demand for residential and commercial construction will expand significantly the property tax base in California. Such a building boom will be but the leading edge in a surge of economic activity that will, in turn, produce more income, sales and other tax revenues to state and local governments. For example, higher levels of employment among construction workers and among workers in other businesses supporting the building industry will boost directly total income and sales levels in the California economy. In addition, the California economy will benefit by luring economic activity away from other states. With property taxes lower, other businesses will expand existing activities or locate new activities within the State, creating still more jobs, more investment, higher real wages, and a new, higher equilibrium level of economic activity.

Finally, Proposition 13 is expected to reduce significantly the level of government expenditure for social welfare programs. The improved economic performance of the State implies directly higher levels of employment, and lower levels of state expenditures for unemployment, rent subsidies, aid to families with dependent children, medical and other social welfare programs.

THE NET REVENUE EFFECT: AN ESTIMATE

In order to estimate the impact of a property tax cut in California, a cross-section of twenty states was analysed for the impact of changes in property taxes and, separately, all other taxes on the relative growth in personal income between 1965 and 1975. The twenty states with the largest property tax revenues accruing to state and local governments were used in the sample (Table 1).

Theoretically, any increase in a marginal tax rate in one state relative to other states would slow economic activity and result in a lower aggregate per-

TABLE 1
Tax Revenues and Personal Income ($ million)

	1975			1965		
	Property Taxes	Other Taxes	Personal Income	Property Taxes	Other Taxes	Personal Income
California	7,909	10,493	138,719	3,325	3,398	59,817
New York	6,681	11,894	118,248	2,872	3,854	58,568
Illinois	3,131	5,007	75,798	1,429	1,406	34,837
New Jersey	3,019	2,289	49,591	1,170	651	22,395
Michigan	2,671	3,572	54,463	1,059	1,322	25,389
Massachusetts	2,509	2,233	35,156	930	685	16,408
Texas	2,343	3,961	68,327	979	1,206	24,531
Ohio	2,176	3,568	61,981	1,195	1,113	29,126
Pennsylvania	1,931	5,596	69,642	956	1,867	31,788
Florida	1,359	2,998	46,320	507	846	14,319
Wisconsin	1,249	2,064	25,640	582	701	11,368
Indiana	1,229	1,851	29,602	616	640	13,713
Connecticut	1,088	1,069	21,086	431	394	9,864
Minnesota	908	2,054	22,597	563	501	9,494
Missouri	876	1,615	26,023	401	600	11,871
Maryland	871	2,111	26,117	377	542	10,561
Washington	815	1,580	22,341	285	594	8,729
Georgia	800	1,702	24,734	255	577	9,432
Virginia	782	2,014	28,774	300	538	10,890
Iowa	754	1,075	16,783	429	333	7,441

Source: Data from Bureau of Census and Bureau of Economic Analysis. Compiled by H. C. Wainwright & Co., June 1978.

sonal income. Thus, the states with the largest increase in marginal tax rates would be expected to have the smallest growth in personal income over the ten year period. Consistent data on marginal tax rates were not available. So, changes in the level of tax revenues as a percent of total personal income, the "tax burden," were used as a proxy for changes in tax rates. This analysis suggests that, on average:

- For each 1 percentage point increase in the property tax burden, personal income drops about 16% below its no-tax-increase level.

- For each 1 percentage point increase in the other tax burden, personal income drops about 17½% below its no-tax-increase level.

The actual and predicted levels of personal income in 1975, based on 1965 personal income levels for each of the states, are summarized in Figure 1. If the predicted and actual 1975 levels of personal income are the same, the point will fall on the solid line. If the predicted level was less than actual, the point is below the line and *vice versa*.

The closeness of the fit is striking given the many variables not quantified in the analysis—such as the differences in climates, average age of plant and equipment, skill of labor force, changes in tax burdens of neighboring states,

FIGURE 1
1975 Total Personal Income by State: Actual vs. Expected

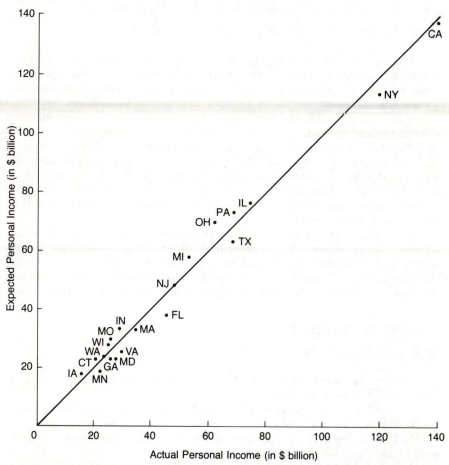

Note: Expected Income in 1975 equals Actual Income in 1965 multiplied by expected growth given the change in tax rates during that period. Expected growth is computed from the equation described in the text.

and wide variations in the distribution of state and local expenditures among such competing budget items as schools, police and fire departments, welfare and social services, unemployment compensation and highways. Nearly 40% of the difference between states in the growth of aggregate personal income over this period can be explained by the change in the burden of property and other taxes on personal income.

Based on this ten year statistical relationship, passage of the Jarvis-Gann initiative could mean:

- a $110 billion increase in personal income above where it otherwise would be;

- a $4 billion loss in property tax revenue instead of the forecasted $7 billion loss;

- an $8 billion increase in other state and local tax revenues;

- a $4 billion net increase in total state and local tax revenues.

The increases in the property tax base, personal income, and other tax revenues would flow, in part, from improved allocations of existing capital and labor within California made possible by the reduction in the property tax wedge and increased incentives to work and invest. In addition, increased amounts of both capital and labor can be expected to flow to California from other states and abroad.

Therefore, we believe that passage of Proposition 13 could boost aggregate personal income in California $20 billion or more above what it otherwise would be during the next twelve months; that nearly half of the income and tax revenue impact will occur within the next two years; and that the full estimated $110 billion increment to aggregate personal income in California will be realized within ten years.

As a direct consequence of this growth in economic activity, social welfare spending should decline. The combined effect implies that California governments would, in short order, be back in surplus, and that there is little cause for sharp reduction in spending, especially for such constitutionally mandated programs as schools and essential services such as fire and police protection.

INVESTMENT IMPLICATIONS

With the passage of Proposition 13:

1. Immigration of capital and labor into California from the rest of the nation and abroad will accelerate.

2. State or municipal bonds funded only by specific property tax revenues most likely will be impaired.

3. The quality of State and municipal bonds collateralized by general revenues most likely will be enhanced.

4. Sales and profits of corporations dependent on the California market or with large operations in the State (e.g., construction companies, banks, retail, wholesale, and industrial goods suppliers) will improve, on average, relative to all other companies.

5. A real world test of the idea that cutting tax rates can lead to higher tax revenues is now forthcoming. Once this concept embodied in the *Laffer Curve* is better understood and accepted, the probability of tax rate cuts at both the national and local level will increase. The improved outlook for lower tax rates alone will affect positively stock and bond prices.

"Meat-Axe Radicalism" in California

WALTER HELLER

Walter Heller compares and contrasts the two property tax relief measures that appeared on the June ballot in California—Proposition 13 (Jarvis-Gann) and Proposition 8. He views Proposition 8 as "a constructive alternative" that would have provided the needed tax relief while not causing severe cutbacks in services. Proposition 13 comes under fire particularly for its built-in tax limit and failure to include a requirement for renter relief.

The property tax revolt is reaching white-heat intensity. How else would a radical measure like the Jarvis-Gann initiative (Proposition 13) have a good chance of passing in California tomorrow even though a superior and more moderate alternative (Proposition 8) appears on the same ballot?

The apparent determination of California voters "to send them a message" through Proposition 13—at a tax loss of $7 billion a year, perhaps the most costly message in history—has evidently caught the country's imagination: . . .

Item: Just last week, 50% of the respondents in a Minnesota Poll survey voiced approval of the Jarvis-Gann amendment (even though the significant property tax relief has already been voted in Minnesota).

Item: Whether one appears before audiences in Norfolk, or New Orleans, or New York, one of the first questions from the floor concerns Jarvis-Gann.

THE ESSENTIAL ELEMENTS

Yet [the Jarvis-Gann amendment is] a seriously and perhaps fatally flawed proposal. The essential elements of Proposition 13 are as follows:

- It slashes the maximum property tax rate up to 1% of the full cash value (1975–76 assessed value) of real property.

- Assessed values may not be increased more than 2% per year except on property that changes hands.

- At the state level, the majority vote is replaced by a two-thirds vote requirement for new or increased taxes. New taxes based on the value or sale of real property are banned.

- No new substitute taxes can be levied at the local level unless approved by two-thirds of the "qualified electors."

Far from being a constructive "experiment in democracy," Proposition 13 would help dig the grave of local self-government. It would rip the heart out of

Walter Heller, " 'Meat-Axe Radicalism' in California," *The Wall Street Journal*, June 5, 1978, p. 18. Reprinted by permission of the author and *The Wall Street Journal*, ©Dow Jones & Company, Inc., 1978. All Rights Reserved.

local finances by chopping away nearly 60% of the $12 billion of local property taxes. And by freezing assessments (except for the glacial thaw of 2% a year) and requiring a two-thirds majority of all electors for any new taxes, it would bar any life-giving local tax transplant.

Chaotic cuts in local school, hospital, police and fire services would be the order of the day. Indeed, to meet advance-notice requirements, wholesale dismissal letters have already gone out to a large number of teachers in San Diego, Los Angeles, and other communities. The strangled local governments would be forced to turn to the state for fiscal handouts, not just from existing surpluses, but permanently. State sales and income taxes would have to be boosted.

Apart from this erosion of local self-reliance, since when is it good democratic practice to imbed in the Constitution measures that prevent elected representatives from responding to the changing needs of the electorate? Indeed, under Jarvis-Gann the fiscal noose would grow tighter and tighter. Rolling back assessed values to 1975–76 would cut the initial effective rate on today's values to perhaps three-quarters of 1%. And with market values of real estate growing at even a "modest" 10% a year, the 2% limit on growth in assessed values would cut the property tax ceiling to less than one-half of 1% of market values within a few years. By putting legislators in such fiscal irons, the new constitutional tax limit would enfeeble government and weaken democracy.

Even apart from broader questions of fiscal management and philosophy, the effects of Jarvis-Gann would range from capricious to deplorable.

The provision freezing assessed values to the 1975–76 (except for the token 2% annual rise) for properties that do not change ownership, while permitting properties that change hands to be appraised at the full market value at the time of transfer, is anomalous, not to say weird. Two properties of identical market value could have sharply different assessed values if one of them were sold after March 1, 1975. This unequal treatment of equals flies directly in the face of constitutional tax principles. And the lock-in effect, the restriction of mobility, the inequities between those who can stay and those who have to go, make this provision a nightmare.

Nothing in Proposition 13 requires a pass-through of benefits from landlords to renters. And the slow and viscous process of competition in housing offers little promise of relief to renters. Those who are too poor to own their own homes take it on the chin twice—once as renters and again as recipients of curtailed local services.

To the surprise of many, the biggest bonanza under Jarvis-Gann goes to Uncle Sam. A UCLA study shows that $2.7 billion of the $7 billion denied local governments would end up in the U.S. Treasury as a result of shrunken income tax deductions.

The UCLA econometric model also shows a loss of 300,000 local jobs, plus 100,000 private jobs, under Proposition 13—hardly the economic tonic that proponents promise.

A CONSTRUCTIVE ALTERNATIVE

Fortunately, Californians will have a constructive alternative when they enter the voting booths tomorrow, namely, Proposition 8, which would activate Senate Bill 1. Under the prod of Jarvis-Gann, the legislature passed and Governor

Brown signed SB-1 providing: (1) a 30% immediate property tax cut for homeowners, to be financed primarily from the state's $3 billion budget surplus; (2) a curb on local property tax revenues by limiting their growth to the rate of inflation (specifically the rise in the GNP deflator) plus taxes on new construction, a combination that would save taxpayers about $1 billion a year by 1983; (3) added relief of about $175 million a year for renters, together with the liberalized relief for senior citizens; and (4) an implicit curb on new state spending by dedication of the existing state surplus to property tax relief, plus an explicit curb by a complex formula tying the rate of growth in state tax revenues to the rate of growth in state personal income.

Thus, Proposition 8 offers sizable relief for hard-pressed homeowners without crippling effects on local self-government, on essential services, and on the California economy.

But there is an electoral booby-trap. If *both* 8 and 13 pass, 8 is preempted and 13 prevails. And since 13 is self-contained while 8 is a bare-bones authorization that requires a knowledge of SB-1, the balance may be swung by ignorance.

And speaking of ignorance, or misunderstanding, one finds that a blizzard of higher assessment notices has generated a last-minute surge of sentiment for 13 even though much of the impact of higher valuation will be offset by lower tax rates.

Clearly, governments the country over need to be brought to book, they need to deliver more value per dollar of tax, and they need to deliver excessive tax dollars back to the taxpayer. But all of that can be readily granted without committing fiscal hara-kiri.

One has to hope that Californians will send their message to government via the moderation of Proposition 8 rather than the meat-axe radicalism of Proposition 13.

Aftershocks from the Great California Taxquake

JOHN QUIRT

This post-Proposition 13 analysis explores the many issues that have arisen as a result of its passage. A comparison of the actual cut-backs versus predicted cut-backs is included, along with a discussion of the close attention being given the selected allocation of businesses' tax savings and the pressure on landlords to pass on their tax savings to renters. The article also outlines the tax cut's various implications for the housing market.

When California voters approved Proposition 13 in June, they turned a state with a long tradition of innovation into a new kind of economic laboratory. The constitutional amendment they adopted—rechanneling billions of dollars from the public to the private sector through a 57 percent property-tax cut—has already created a thicket of anomalies and puzzles that seem strange even by California standards. Myths propounded during the hot, emotional campaign have been demolished. But the passage of the proposition has confronted business with a host of new and unexpected dilemmas. How companies meet these challenges will have a considerable impact on the state's political temper and economic climate for several years to come.

The largest voter-imposed tax cut in U.S. history, Proposition 13 will save California property owners about $7 billion next year. It will lower their tax rates from 3 percent to 1 percent of market value, roll back the base year for assessments to fiscal 1975–76 (except when property is new or changes hands), and limit future increases in assessments to a mere 2 percent a year.

For a commercial building whose assessment has risen from $700,000 in 1976 to $1 million today, Proposition 13 would bring a tax saving of more than $20,000. For the 55 percent of Californians who occupy their own homes, the average tax cut will be about $600. To safeguard these savings, the measure requires a two-thirds vote of the legislature, instead of a simple majority, to impose any new or higher state taxes. Local governments face an equally high hurdle: voters must ratify any new taxes by a two-thirds margin.

A $5-BILLION BAILOUT

For state and local governments, 13 was a battle with middle-class homeowners incensed over soaring tax bills (40 percent a year increases had become common) and profligate government spending. Many public officials accepted defeat with ill grace. Soon after the election, some libraries stopped lending books.

John Quirt, "Aftershocks from the Great California Taxquake." Reprinted from the September 25, 1978 issue of FORTUNE Magazine, pp. 75–84, by special permission; ©1978 Time Inc.

In many cities, summer-school classes were canceled. Hysterical pre-election warnings echoed again: schools might not reopen in the fall, and there would have to be massive cutbacks in police and fire protection.

As it turns out, essential public services have not been emasculated. Governor Jerry Brown and the legislature bailed out local governments with nearly $5 billion from the state's embarrassingly large $6.6-billion surplus. (Had they used some of that money earlier to lower taxes, 13 might not have passed.) Only about 20,000 public employees have been laid off, and some of these are gradually being rehired.

Throughout the state, governmental units have begun a recalcitrant adjustment to an era when revenue from property taxes and tax-increment bonds will be less bountiful. Most spending cuts so far have been small, under 10 percent on average. The San Francisco Museum of Modern Art, for instance, has had its budget trimmed by only 5 percent. Nearly two-thirds of the state's school districts have as much or a bit more money this fall than a year ago; others must manage with slightly less. Many special districts, which handle such functions as irrigation, hospitals, and water supply, have been hit harder. Even after the infusion of state funds, a Marin County mosquito-control district suffered a one-third cut in its $471,000 budget.

After opposing 13 during the campaign as a "rip-off" and a potential "disaster," Governor Brown did an instant flip-flop after the proposition passed by a two-to-one margin, and declared his support for a smaller public sector. He has frozen the salaries of the state's 190,000 employees and forbidden new hiring. In addition, Brown and the legislature have killed half a dozen new programs, including one to buy a share in a communications satellite.

But waste has been chopped only gently from the $40-billion combined budgets of the state, its fifty-eight counties, 417 cities, 1,046 school districts, and 4,710 special districts. Three months after an election that supposedly gave the bureaucracy a new sense of frugality, hundreds of high-ranking public servants are still commuting to work in government cars at taxpayers' expense. Public-works spending is continuing almost as if 13 had lost.

Proposition 13 has become even more popular with California voters than it was before the election, according to a public-opinion poll taken by the Los Angeles *Times* in late June. Nevertheless, school, county, and city officials, backed by public-employee unions, are battling to have the measure scrapped on constitutional grounds. Last month, the state supreme court began hearing arguments on three such suits.

AN AWKWARD BLUNDERBUSS

Proposition 13 is certainly vulnerable to legal attack. Co-authored by Howard Jarvis, seventy-five, a crusty anti-tax zealot, and Paul Gann, sixty-six, a retired real-estate man, the eight-paragraph measure is an awkwardly phrased blunderbuss. The state constitution stipulates that an initiative placed on the ballot by voters' petitions may cover only one topic. Opponents contend that 13 violates that proviso by limiting assessments *and* making it harder for the legislature to pass new taxes. By exempting new and resold property from the rollback to 1975–76 assessment levels, critics argue, the proposition may violate the equal-protection clause of the Fourteenth Amendment to the U.S. Constitution, because it could impose substantially different taxes on two identical houses. In rebuttal, John J. Klee Jr., an assistant attorney general, argued before the court that all of 13's provisions relate to "the common purpose of lowering taxes." As for the equal-protection issue, he pointed out that older laws already allow property to be taxed at varying levels.

Not least among the aftershocks of the great taxquake is the intemperate animosity still displayed by both 13's winners and losers. The seven supreme court justices have been threatened with recall, defeat at the polls, and even physical harm if they overturn the measure. On the other hand, hundreds of state workers picketed the state capitol in June, jeering, hissing, and booing Governor Brown, who vetoed a bill giving them only a small pay increase.

Tenant groups have been assailing apartment-house owners who fail to use their tax savings to lower rents. Joined by Howard Jarvis, the governor has exhorted landlords to reduce rents and warned them that they face rent-control legislation that would force rollbacks unless they share the tax savings.

The warning has been heeded by dozens of large landlords. L. B. Nelson Corp., for example, last month began passing along its $150,000 tax savings by rebating between $15 and $35 per month to 636 tenants in Alameda, Walnut Creek, and Mountain View. But many owners of small apartment buildings are balking. Their stand prompted the Los Angeles city council to vote last month to roll back rents to May 31 levels and prohibit increases for six months.

THREATS TO THE GOODIES

If business in general were to feel the heat now focused on landlords, it could lose most or all of its tax savings. Business has the biggest stake in 13: it stands to receive roughly $4 billion, or a little over half of the total tax cut. More than $400 million of that is going to big utilities and transportation companies. Southern Pacific, the state's largest private landholder, expects its property-tax bill to drop from $35 million to $19 million.

The Bank of America expects to save around $13 million and Atlantic-Richfield $14 million. But because of lower realty-tax deductions, about half of the corporate tax saving will be paid out in higher income taxes. (For the same reason, homeowners on average will be able to keep only about three-quarters of their saving.)

Utilities and transportation companies face no quandary over what to do with their extra money. They are required by the state utilities commission to pass the savings along to customers. Pacific Telephone & Telegraph, for instance, filed a $94-million rate reduction that would cut monthly phone bills for residential customers between 25 cents and 60 cents.

Most other businessmen want to treat their tax saving like any other reduced cost, and use it to increase profits, retire debt, or help meet other corporate goals, even if that means investing the money outside California. But they are starting to feel political pressure to earmark it for community projects or to create jobs and help the state's economy. Brown has told them they have a "moral obligation" to do so. Civic officials are calling on them to share their "windfall" with the public through increased support for cultural and recreational programs. And community activist groups are besieging them with requests to help the disadvantaged and the poor.

Howard Jarvis evaluates the significance of all of this pressure in characteristically blunt terms. "Businessmen are really stupid," he says, "if they fail to realize that after landlords they may be the next target. They had better do something special with their savings. I'll be kicked in the head for saying that, but I know something about California's political mood. And if businessmen can't figure out the message, they deserve whatever they get."

"A TIME BOMB FOR BUSINESS"

What they are likely to get, if the public mood turns solidly against them, is another amendment to the state constitution reducing business's share of the tax cut or wiping it out entirely. California voters rejected a constitutional amendment to give property-tax relief only to homeowners (Proposition 8) in June, and an attempt to put a similar measure on the ballot this fall failed last month in the legislature. Further attempts, though, are almost certain to be made before the June, 1980, election.

Under these circumstances, says Lester Korn, Los Angeles-based president of Korn/Ferry, the executive-search firm, "Proposition 13 has become sort of a time bomb for business. Businessmen must decide how to share their tax cut and do it promptly—or they're likely to discover the decision has been made for them."

A few small companies have tried to get out in front of the issue by announcing that their tax break is being passed along to employees as wage increases, or to customers through price cuts. A handful of other businesses have disclosed special hiring programs or plans to use part of the money to fund community projects. In Thousand Oaks, a suburban community northwest of Los Angeles, several firms have announced plans to create a $1-million fund with tax savings and give the interest to local officials to help pay for government services. "I'm not sure business actually deserved to be included in 13," says Nathan Shapell, a prominent housing developer who is participating in the plan. "And it's apparent to me that we do have an obligation to help out with at least part of the money." Most companies, however, are waiting to see exactly how much their tax cut amounts to before deciding what to do with it.

Nearly all of California's major industries are affected by 13, but housing is touched most extensively. Home prices in the state rose astronomically between mid-1975 and last June; in southern California the median price of existing one-family houses climbed from $43,000 to $70,107. Diligent assessors reflected the increases through prompt reassessments. It was the resulting leap in tax bills that produced such widespread outrage, giving the Jarvis-Gann initiative broad support. Now Proposition 13 is turning out to have repercussions on housing that are both positive and negative.

On the plus side, it eliminates uncertainty about future tax increases as a disincentive to buy. And it lowers the ongoing cost of home ownership by an average of about $50 a month for a $50,000 house, a decline that should enable at least 100,000 more Californians to qualify for home loans. Explains Anthony Frank, chairman of United Financial Corp. of California, a San Francisco-based savings and loan holding company: "The $50 translates into $2,400 more borrowing power for lower-middle-income people who haven't been able to qualify. It's got to provide some stimulus in the starter market. And this will mean more loans to first-time buyers."

A good case can be made that California's housing boom will be extended not only because of those newly qualified borrowers but also because some 200,000 people a year are pouring into the state—more than double the net in-migration rate during the early 1970's. Apartment vacancy rates are low— under 3 percent in most big metropolitan areas—and many new arrivals find themselves forced to buy whether they want to or not.

FALLING SALES, BUT RISING PRICES

On the minus side, the clamor for rent control is inhibiting new investment in apartments. As a consequence, a widely forecast increase in the construction of rental housing (which, in the long run, would have slowed the pace of rent increases by increasing the supply of available units) seems unlikely to begin any time soon. Proposition 13 has also undercut the resale market for existing homes. The provision permitting reassessments when properties change hands is discouraging many owners from trading up to bigger and better dwellings. Volume in this part of the realty business has slowed in some areas, and homes in the $100,000 to $200,000 bracket, which sold quickly a year ago, now remain on the market for several months. Property prices are still climbing, partly because lower taxes are being capitalized into higher values. That trend will further deter potential buyers.

The housing and real-estate industries are being pinched by new or higher fees, many of dubious legality, that have been imposed by local governments facing a big drop in property-tax revenue. The city of Redding, for example, has raised its "construction tax" to some $2,000 per house for parks, storm drains, and other services. Oceanside has more than doubled its zoning fees. Citizens Savings & Loan, which not only finances homes throughout the state but also builds them in forty-four locations, figures that increased fees add up to $2,484 per home; these extra costs have completely wiped out the property-tax savings on all of its seventy-nine branch offices.

The outburst of fee raising is most evident in outlying communities where public facilities have to be built from scratch. If, as seems logical, developers turn away from such places, urban sprawl may slow down. One consequence might be more private investment in the inner cities. They will need it more than ever, because many urban-redevelopment projects are being stymied by Proposition 13's limit on assessment increases; it will keep taxes on such projects too low to pay off the bonds to finance them.

Other California businesses also have been hit by higher municipal levies. Beverly Hills, for example, sharply increased its annual business-license fees just before 13 took effect July 1; on a commercial rental property with $500,000 a year in gross receipts, the rise is 1,800 percent to $11,750. In several cities, lawsuits have been filed by business groups who contend that increases imposed between June 6 and July 1 violate the intent of the initiative.

Proposition 13 will give retail sales a lift because it will increase many consumers' aftertax incomes. And the billions being injected into the spending stream from the budget surplus, which was a drag on the state's economy, will also stimulate business activity. California doesn't need much of a lift right now. Key industries such as aerospace are booming. About 500,000 new jobs will be generated in California this year, enough to absorb most laid-off government

California's Economic Outlook:
A Lift, Then a Letdown

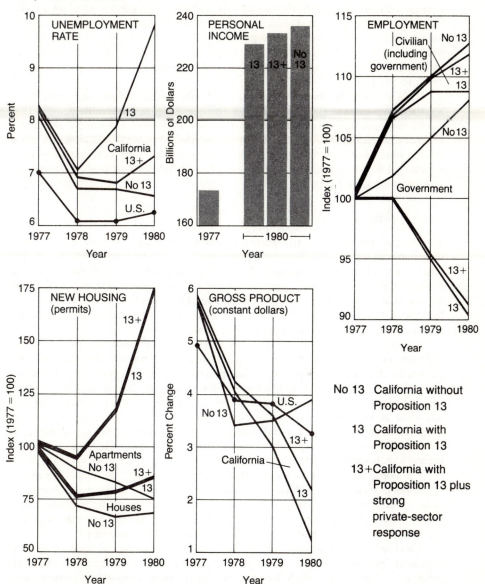

No 13   California without
        Proposition 13

   13   California with
        Proposition 13

13+ California with
        Proposition 13 plus
        strong
        private-sector
        response

Using its econometric model of the California economy, the U.C.L.A. Graduate School of Management has produced three intriguingly different forecasts through 1980. They indicate that the housing industry will be the chief beneficiary of Proposition 13; provided no rent controls are imposed, a 50 percent increase in housing starts is expected by 1980. The rest of the state's economy will get a lift at first, then grow more slowly than if 13 had not passed. If business responds strongly to the property-tax cut by accelerating its job-creating investments, it could partly offset anticipated layoffs of state and municipal workers. Even with a strong response by the private sector, U.C.L.A. predicts California's output of goods and services will expand less rapidly than the G.N.P. in 1980.

workers. The seasonally adjusted jobless rate in July was 7.8 percent, down from 8.2 percent a year earlier. It traditionally runs slightly above the national average, mainly because of the steady influx of job seekers from other states. But according to the U.C.L.A. Graduate School of Management's forecast, the rate for the full year 1978 will be 6.9 percent, only two-tenths of a percent higher than it would have been without 13, thanks mainly to the state's job-saving aid to localities. Personal income in the state is expected to rise 11 percent from 1977, to $193 billion.

This prosperity should continue well into 1979, leaving the state with another surplus next June of perhaps $5 billion, despite the sizable pre-election cut in state income taxes that was headed for legislative approval last month. Most of that money, too, will no doubt be distributed to local governments. After June, 1980, state surpluses, generated by income and sales taxes, may well be smaller. If so, local budgets will have to be cut further and more government employees will be laid off.

A TEST FOR ECONOMIC THEORY

The crucial question for the state's economy, therefore, is how boldly businessmen will respond to 13 by increasing their job-creating investments. On this topic economists differ. Arthur Laffer of the University of Southern California estimates that the property-tax cut will trigger enough additional private investment and spending over the next decade to lift personal income in the state by $110 billion more than it would have risen without the initiative. About half of that gain, he says, should come in the next two years.

Laffer expects the budget surplus to rise, and unemployment to fall, as California's economy flourishes and generates additional tax revenues. And he contends that this will begin to happen so fast that even the decline in property-tax revenue during the current fiscal year, ending next June, will be smaller than the widely predicted $7 billion. Laffer is the country's leading advocate of the theory that a big cut in tax rates can spark a boom of such magnitude that government will eventually gain revenue instead of losing it (see "Professor Laffer's Famous Curve," FORTUNE, April 10). He considers 13 an important though imperfect test of his theory.

"It would have been better to reduce income-tax rates," he says. "But this is still a fairly good test. California is a high-tax state, and the effect on incentives to invest and spend will be much greater here than it would be in many other places. Also, our surplus is available to help out until the tax cut becomes self-financing. So I'm relatively sanguine about the outcome of 13."

Economist Larry Kimbell, director of U.C.L.A. forecasting models, is considerably less optimistic. He predicts that unemployment will rise to about 10 percent of California's work force in two years unless business creates some 200,000 new industrial jobs and 90,000 in retailing, or enough to offset anticipated reductions in public employment. Even if that happens, Kimbell believes the 1980 jobless rate will be no lower than this year's. The use of the surplus to bail out California cities, in his view, may have merely postponed additional government layoffs. Says Kimbell: "It's doubtful if we can make up all of the lost tax revenue as instantaneously as Laffer suggests. His argument is credible if we are talking five or ten years, but probably not before that."

MORE APPEAL TO INVESTORS?

Kimbell and Laffer, in other words, agree that 13 should spur the private sector, but disagree over the timing, and over how strong and lasting the stimulus will be. Neither economist assumes that business will make special efforts to set aside tax savings for use in the state. Says Laffer: "What we want to find out is whether higher rates of return can help attract more investment capital from within and from outside the state. We've had a serious business-climate problem here, and it's one the initiative could ameliorate because capital can move fairly freely across state lines."

Ultimately, business's response to 13 will be greatly influenced by its perception of whether state and local governments are getting the tax revolt's message and curbing their easy-spending ways. As economist Walter Hoadley, executive vice president of the Bank of America, puts it: "The real issue is whether business concludes that 13 is the start of a new, more responsible fiscal policy in the state. And a key question that will be answered over the next year or so is whether it has become politically safe to restrict spending and adopt budgets for programs that take proper care of the underprivileged but not the chiselers and cheaters."

A WARNING FOR "DUMB POLITICIANS"

In California, the most likely way of achieving large spending cutbacks is through initiative petitions that bypass the legislature to put policy issues on the ballot. Howard Jarvis, who complains that general-spending limitations can be easily circumvented, has begun studying a variety of other ways of using the initiative process to force cutbacks. "We should give the politicians some time to do their job," he says. "But they're pretty dumb and they may not respond adequately. If they don't, I've got four million votes in my pocket that I can deliver to secure the gains won by 13. And I'll do it again if I have to."

Four million votes is nearly two-thirds of the total turnout in the June election, and the prospect of Jarvis's legion of supporters marching to the polls behind him again—with a new thunderbolt for government—logically should bestir state and local lawmakers toward making sensible spending reductions to ward off further draconian initiatives. Proposition 13 has left a lot of unfinished business. The chief unresolved question is whether Jarvis and his allies can permanently force the state and local governments to play a smaller and less costly role in California's affairs.

Voting for Capitalism

JOHN A. DAVENPORT

This final article provides a fitting conclusion by relating the tax revolt in California to the variety of tax limitation measures under consideration in other states and on the federal level. John A. Davenport captures the spirit of this movement to restructure our tax system in a fashion designed to strengthen and expand our economy.

As a windup to his justly famous classes in sociology, the late great William Graham Sumner of Yale was wont to conclude his final lecture with the injunction: *"Gentlemen, get capital."* In seeking an interpretive handle for what is commonly called the great tax revolt of 1978, this mundane (some might say obscene) injunction of New Haven's sage comes echoing to mind. Since Sumner's day, many an American has followed his prudent advice, with the result that, contrary to Marxian predictions of a society with a dwindling number of fat cats at the top and a multiplying revolutionary proletariat at the bottom, the U.S. is a diamond-shaped society with a vast and industrious middle class giving ballast to its political economy.

THE VOX MEDIORUM IS HEARD

This property-owning class, which might be called the huge Sumner constituency, by now includes most members of what used to be referred to as the working class. And it is precisely this class that is today aroused about exorbitant taxes of all kinds, which are eating not only into their income, but into their hard-won savings and capital. What this *vox mediorum* is saying to government at all levels is: get out of our pocketbooks and give us back control of our own resources. What the middle class is also saying, or rather assuming, is that if the load of government could be lightened, if young and old were allowed not only to get capital but to keep it, the private economy could propel the country into a new era of expansion.

In analyzing this revolt of the middle class, however, it is necessary to distinguish between two different yet compounding factors. The first is the sheer weight of the tax load, which, counting federal, state, and local levies, absorbs over 34 percent of the net national product and makes May—once the symbol of Communist revolution—notable as the first month when the average U.S. citizen ceases to work for the government and begins to work for himself.

Yet this load of taxation might never have had its explosive consequences had it not been for the appearance of the greatest tax collector of them all,

John A. Davenport, "Voting for Capitalism." Reprinted from the July 17, 1978 issue of FORTUNE Magazine, pp. 46–48, by special permission; ©1978 Time Inc.

namely inflation. When inflation is running at a 7 percent rate, it exacts a tax of 140 percent on the widow with money in the savings bank at 5 percent. Wage earners who get cost-of-living increases find themselves pushed into higher brackets of a progressive income tax. While government expenditures are largely indexed for surging prices, the taxpayer has had no such happy dispensation. The ultimate beneficiary of inflation is thus government itself. Yet government is also the principal cause of inflation since at the federal level it controls the printing presses. The process is thus self-perpetuating.

THE ROAR FROM CALIFORNIA

At some point, this vicious cycle must be broken, and the means thereto may not always be as prettily calculated as a conclave of economists might like. In California, where the roar for tax relief has been loudest, the voters seized the obvious weapon at hand, a dramatic slash in property taxes. Their behavior is not surprising, for California perfectly illustrates how the double scoop of taxes and inflation eats into middle-class substance. In California, assessments of real estate are methodically revised each year to conform to true market values. With inflation and speculation inexorably driving up those values, Californians found the tax bite intolerable. The overwhelming passage of Proposition 13, which has the effect of cutting property taxes by 57 percent, was an angry but effective way to get out of at least part of this bind, and clear warning to Sacramento to tighten up on its spending habits.

PUTTING ON A CAP

This is likewise the message of innumerable tax-limitation committees, which are sprouting like dandelions all across the broad land with the objective of capping state and, indeed, federal taxes and expenditures. Tennessee has already amended its state constitution to limit the growth of state spending to the actual growth of its economy—a more rational approach than California's single smashing attack on local real-estate taxes. As a matter of fact, California, in Governor Reagan's day, came within an ace of approving a spending cap, and petitions for doing this are now circulating in Colorado and Michigan. The groups promoting these amendments are as obscure as Howard Jarvis used to be. Like the California tax rebels, they have concluded that the legislative branch of government is no match for all the special-interests promoting worthy social causes, and that the voters can impose their will only by slashing government revenues or fixing iron lids on spending.

HOW TO HELP THE POOR

It is unfortunate that spokesmen for some of the special-interest groups, including the leaders of several prominent black organizations, have leaped to the conclusion that the principal result of the tax revolt, and perhaps its unspoken intention, is to fatten middle-class pocketbooks at the expense of the poor. No doubt some people do feel that way, and without doubt those people voted for Proposition 13. What most people are beefing about, however, is not the cost of helping others but the inefficiency of the way we do it.

It has become quite common for young unemployed blacks to spend a year of labor and hope in one or another of the publicly funded employment-and-training programs only to be dumped out at the other end no better prepared to get and hold a job in the private sector. Looked at in the larger scale of the economy as a whole, the government, by stifling the private sector through excessive taxation and raising the minimum wage, has been creating unemployment on the one hand and trying to float it off with public programs and deficit financing on the other.

The positive side of the antitax movement is its assumption that if the grip of government is relaxed, the juices of capitalism will flow into productive effort—creating real rather than make-work jobs. This assumption surfaces most plainly in some of the intricate tax arguments being heard in Washington, a city that may soon have as many economists as lawyers. One of the new games in town is playing with the "Laffer curve," named after an economist at the University of Southern California, Arthur B. Laffer. Its basic, incontrovertible proposition is that at some point higher tax rates begin to strangle economic activity and so produce lower, not higher, revenues. Just at what point this effect takes place depends upon one's econometric model—and Washington has plenty of these.

But Laffer's analysis has already made a deep impression on politicians of all stripes, notably on Congressman Jack Kemp of Hamburg, N.Y. . . . He argues that Republicans should abandon the old Hoover doctrine of balancing the budget first, and then maybe thinking about tax cutting. Instead he would slash tax rates 30 percent across the board, confident that increased revenues would then roll in, a proposal whose time has not yet quite come.

THE CONGRESSMAN FROM OSHKOSH

To the discomfiture of the Carter Administration, however, which has been pressing for a hike in the capital gains tax, respectable economic models do seem to indicate that a substantial cut in that particular tax would be a boon to the Treasury as well as to the taxpayer. By now, close to a majority in Congress has rallied behind the Steiger amendment, which would roll back the tax on corporate capital gains from 30 percent to 25 percent, and likewise restore the 25 percent tax cap on individual capital gains, in place of the newfangled hat under which some of our richer citizens pay close to 50 percent when they sell stocks or other capital assets.

A less likely proposal to gain wide support, given the long-standing propensity of politicians to "soak the rich," could scarcely be imagined. Yet wispish William A. Steiger, an obscure Republican Congressman from Oshkosh, has emerged as something of a Capitol Hill hero whose ideas (perhaps in compromised form) are all but sure to go into any tax legislation.

Behind the Steiger firecracker are not just millionaires and timber barons but also a broad spectrum of expert opinion that, long before the current tax revolt, had begun to worry about the fundamental health of the economy. This concern centers on the fact that the tax structure is not just oppressive in its total weight. It is tilted heavily to favor current consumption and to discourage savings, investment, and capital formation, on which productivity and real growth depend.

TAXES ON LOSSES

Of all the various taxes involved in the decapitation of enterprise, the one on capital gains is surely the oddest in an age of inflation. Martin Feldstein of Harvard has pointed out that in 1973 individuals paid taxes on some $4.5 billion of nominal gains on the sale of corporate stock. But if the original costs of these shares are adjusted for inflation since their purchase, it turns out that the nominal capital gain was in fact a real capital loss of nearly $1 billion. In the upshot, the Treasury raked in extra millions though people had lost money!

Dr. Richard W. Rahn, executive director of the thriving American Council for Capital Formation (scarcely a name with much sex appeal), has put together all the various levies on corporate capital, and he figures that the total in some cases comes to over 90 percent. No wonder that the U.S., the alleged home of capitalist imperialism, ranks far down the totem pole when it comes to saving and investment, outstripped by Japan, Germany, and even Britain. And other warning signals are flying. Profits, the spark plug of the system, are by no means as flashy as they look. In fact, cash flow (retained earnings plus depreciation) is wholly inadequate to cover the rising costs of replacing plant and equipment.

TURNING TO JAPAN

Cutting the capital-gains tax would not remedy all these problems, but it would be a beginning. It would palpably increase the flow of risk capital badly needed by small and struggling ventures and supplied in the past by the rich (it was J. P. Morgan who helped stake Thomas A. Edison, and frozen orange juice owes a debt to the likes of John Hay Whitney).

Significantly, the American Electronics Association had a hand in formulating the Steiger amendment, and Edwin Zschau, chairman of the association's task force, impressed the House Ways and Means Committee with a personal example of why it is needed. He reported that because of the shortage of venture capital in this country, his own small company, System Industries, recently had to turn to Japan to get the money needed to develop a new ink-jet printer. Zschau may or may not have helped his cause with a song, titled "The Old Risk Capital Blues," which he has been crooning to various groups around Washington:

> We've got those old risk capital blues,
> Folks don't invest, consume's what they choose,
> The gains are what attract 'em
> But not when we high tax 'em
> And there's high risk they could lose.

Besides aiding the small entrepreneur, the Steiger amendment would tend to raise the value of all assets, release "locked in" investors in common stocks, and make it easier for corporations to float new equity issues instead of debt. Finally, the very fact that government was paying some attention to the guts of capitalism—namely, capital itself—would improve the entire financial climate. The argument of Secretary of the Treasury Blumenthal that tinkering with the capital-gains tax "would sharply erode the progressivity and horizontal equity of the income-tax system" is perhaps the best argument for change, since it is progressivity that has got us into a lot of our troubles.

What is needed, in short, is not just a reduction in tax rates but a turnaround in public policy in order to stimulate, rather than penalize, expansion. Since Steiger's is the only bandwagon in town, businessmen have happily clambered aboard, but they would not find it hard to back more far-reaching reforms, such as eliminating the double taxation of dividends (see "A Manifesto for a Tax Revolution," FORTUNE, April, 1977). With inflation continuing and even accelerating, another measure that deserves urgent consideration is the indexing of the tax system to adjust for the effects of rising prices—a sound idea that has, in the language of the financial markets, been "crowded out" by more dramatic developments.

Indexing would eliminate the injustice Feldstein describes. It would also keep wage earners from being artificially pushed into higher brackets. And it would prevent government, the engine of inflation, from reaping its rewards. Once government is stripped of the inflationary increment in revenues—the "fiscal dividend," as it used to be called—both the politicians and the voters would be obliged to deal with government spending programs and cut the coat to fit the cloth.

SHOULDERS FOR THE BURDEN

For these programs will have to be faced in the end, as they are now being addressed very painfully in California. The public perception, which helped feed the tax revolt, is that there is a lot of waste in government. Talk of cutting, of course, meets with the direst predictions. "Too bad," the public servants say. "No more cops on the beat, nobody to hold the end of the fire hose—you'll be sorry." But surely this is not the real place to cut. Something can be done about reducing administrative costs and increasing productivity. Beyond this, conscious choices have to be made, and some programs eliminated. At the federal level, the mindless subsidization of special-interest groups (farm price supports, for example) is one place to start. And certainly the times call for restraint at that rising tide of entitlements, which has made the Department of Health, Education, and Welfare a multi-armed and clumsy monster.

Still, at some irreducible point, and whatever the charms of the Laffer curve, the society's real needs will have to be paid for with real money. To cite but one example, military expenditures for the next few years are likelier to rise than fall, and as Adam Smith reminded us long ago, defense takes precedence over opulence. There is, in short, a tax load that has to be borne. We shall bear it the more easily as the great tax revolt is channeled in a way that strengthens the sinews and broadens the shoulders of capitalism.

A 9
B 0
C 1
D 2
E 3
F 4
G 5
H 6
I 7
J 8